FREESIAS

GROWER GUIDE No.1

FREESIAS

Denis Smith

Revised by P. N. Danks

Grower Books · London

Grower Books
50 Doughty Street
London WC1N 2LP

First published 1979
© Grower Books 1979
Reprinted and revised 1985
ISBN 0 901361 78 X

Designed and produced by Sharp Print Management
Printed in Great Britain

Contents

Foreword

The object of this book is to provide flower growers with up-to-date and comprehensive information about all aspects of commercial freesia growing.

The author is grateful to the States of Guernsey Horticultural Advisory Service for allowing the publication of a number of the photographs used, and to the many freesia growers in Guernsey and elsewhere who have contributed greatly to the present state of knowledge of freesia culture.

It is hoped that GROWING FREESIAS, produced from a combination of experimental work and practical experience, will be a useful guide to anyone considering commercial production of this attractive flower.

GUERNSEY, 1979.

1: Introduction

Although freesias have been grown commercially on a small scale in many countries throughout the world, the main centres of production, and therefore of relevant experimental and research work, have always been in Western Europe. The Netherlands easily head the list with an area of about eight hundred acres of glass devoted to freesia cultivation, and producing flowers with a market value of around twenty million pounds sterling each year.

Rather surprisingly, the second largest producer is the tiny Channel Island of Guernsey, which has a total land area of only twenty five square miles. Guernsey has an annual freesia crop value of about three million pounds sterling, produced from one hundred acres of glasshouses. Guernsey's production supplies most of the United Kingdom's requirements for freesias, the UK itself having less than twenty acres of home-grown freesias. Holland's crop is marketed principally throughout mainland Europe.

Other European centres of lesser significance include West Germany and Denmark, while Egypt, Israel, Japan and the USA are the main producers of freesias outside Europe.

Because little written information has been produced on cultural aspects of freesia growing since the 1950's, the general level of knowledge of the crop outside the main centres of production has fallen far behind that which is available within those areas. It is hoped that this book will go some way towards redressing the balance. Tremendous advances in our understanding of the physiological requirements of the freesia plant, and therefore of our ability to grow reliable and profitable crops commercially, have been made in the last quarter of a century, and at the same time the quality of plant material available to growers from plant breeders has improved in proportion.

Freesias are not a particularly demanding crop to grow. The only factor which would appear to stand in the way of their successful cultivation in most flower producing areas is the ability to provide suitable temperature regimes. However, recent developments in the treatment of corms before planting, as described in chapter four, have dramatically reduced the importance of soil temperatures in the growing crop, and it may now be that successful freesia production is a practical proposition for many countries and regions. The general requirements for commercial freesia production are described in chapter two, and it will be seen that freesia growing can be adapted with a little imagination to many climatic areas. Consequently, it is hoped that the cultural information provided here will encourage experimentation in freesia production is such areas, and lead to the wider cultivation of this very attractive flower.

History

The freesia has a relatively short history as a commercial cut-flower crop. The genus was first described, but wrongly classified, as *Gladiolus refractus* by the Austrian botanist Nicolaus von Jacquin in 1790, but it was not until the turn of the present century that a range of wild species material was introduced into Europe from South Africa, the home of the freesia. The first attempts at improving this material by hybridisation were made in 1897 at Kew Gardens, London, prompted by the acquisition of the red-flowered *Freesia Armstrongii*. Previously only yellow and white varieties had been available, so that the possibilities for producing a good range of colours had been limited.

Although these early efforts at plant breeding resulted in material which had little commercial value in itself, they did nevertheless provide a basis on which later workers could build, and the range and quality of hybrid freesias quickly improved. Prominent among these early plant breeders were Dr Ragioneri in Italy and Messrs G.C. van Tubergen in Holland, and it is to these workers, supported by hybridists in England, Germany and the USA, that credit must be given for introducing the first freesia material worthy of consideration for the commercial production of cut flowers.

We will now consider briefly the wild species of freesia from which all modern varieties and strains have been developed. These are all natives of the Cape Province area of South Africa. There is some difference of opinion as to how they should be classified, but there may be only two true species, the yellow *Freesia refracta* and the red-pink *Freesia Armstrongii*. There are several varieties of *Freesia refracta*, making a total of about seventeen sorts, and these include the white-flowered *Freesia refracta alba*, *F. refracta Leichtlinii* with its larger pale yellow flowers blotched with deeper yellow, and the bright yellow *F. refracta odorata*. By breeding between these seventeen wild varieties and then making further crosses among the resultant hybrids the wide range of commercial material which has become available over the last thirty or so years was gradually developed.

Niels Sennels, who as a leading grower in Denmark wrote one of the few authoritative books on the culture of freesias in 1951, described the aims of freesia plant breeding, and then concluded that 'these aims have been achieved, and achieved in such degree, that it is doubtful whether further improvement in form or colour can be made in the future'. He then went on to list nearly forty recommended corm varieties and seed strains. Of these, not one has survived in commercial use to the present day. This shows just how much further progress has in fact been made since that time.

The greatest single step which has been made since the 1950's has been the development of tetraploidy in freesias. Wild species and the older cultivated varieties have two sets of chromosomes in each cell. This is the normal number, and is known as diploidy. If a plant, during the process of seed production, retains twice the normal number of chromosomes it is then referred to as a tetraploid. The most important feature of tetraploid plants is that they are generally larger and stronger than their diploid counterparts. So tetraploid freesias grow more vigorously than diploids, and produce larger flowers on longer stems.

The development of tetraploid freesias has been mainly carried out at the Institute for Plant Breeding at Wageningen in Holland, under the leadership of Dr L.D. Sparnaaij. He has also been responsible for tackling some of the problems associated with this material, notably difficulties of pollination, since tetraploid plants tend to be less prolific seed producers than diploid. However, these problems are now solved, and modern seed strains, which are all tetraploid, are successfully pollinated by introducing hives of bees into the houses used for commercial seed production.

These developments in the production of seed strains for commercial use have been paralleled by similar improvements in corm material. Freesias can be grown either from seed or from corms. Corms can originate by saving the stock from a previous crop grown from seed, in which case they are described as corms-from-seed. Alternatively, a stock of corms may be bulked up vegatatively over a number of years from a single corm selected from a crop. When this is the case, the stock should be referred to as a clone, because it is genetically uniform, but commercially it is usually described as a named variety. A wide range of named variety corms are available to growers, and the majority of these were originally selected and multiplied up in Holland. They vary widely in both quality and production, and it is not practical to include a comprehensive list, as new introductions are continually being made. A list of some of the more established named varieties appears on page 37.

Life cycle

A knowledge of the life cycle of the freesia in its natural habitat is of great value in understanding many of the cultural requirements of the freesia crop, and so a

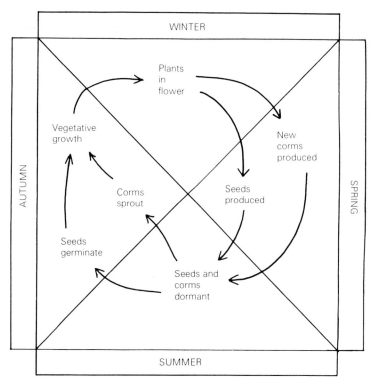

Figure 1 The life cycle of the freesia

brief description of this must now be given. The freesia belongs to the family Iridaceae, and is closely related to both iris and gladioli. A plant can grow either fom a seed or from a corm, and in either case will flower in a single season, after which the foliage dies.

If we start our examination of the life cycle in the South African winter (see figure one), we have a fully grown plant in flower. This plant will set seed, and then begin to die back as summer approaches. During this period after flowering, the new corm which has formed from a thickening of the stem base earlier in the winter begins to mature, and at the same time one or more secondary cormlets may develop around the base of the corm. On the new corm there are a number of buds, any of which may eventually sprout to produce a new plant the following year. However, it is usual for only the terminal bud to sprout, and this in turn inhibits the growth of the lateral buds. If the terminal bud is damaged or destroyed, then one or more of the lateral buds will grow in place of it. Cormlets have only a single bud, and this too will grow into a new plant the following season.

FIG 1
Freesia species (Freesia refracta and F. Armstrongii) in flower. The flowers are small, but delicate, and have a good scent. These plants are part of a collection at the Guernsey Horticultural Advisory Service.

As the leaves of the plant die back during the spring, we are therefore left with a number of seeds, a single corm, and usually one or more cormlets. The corm and cormlets are now dormant and, with the seeds, will remain so during the hot, dry summer months. As autumn approaches and the temperatures fall, the seeds become capable of germination and corm growth will then begin with the arrival of the autumn rains. Germination of the seed had previously been prevented by the high soil temperatures of late summer and by the lack of soil moisture. Premature corm sprouting had been avoided by a mechanism of corm dormancy, whereby the corm requires a long period of high temperatures before active growth is possible.

So as autumn approaches the seeds germinate and grow into plants which will eventually be capable of producing flower buds. The corm and cormlets similarly start into active growth, and the old corm dries up as its nutrients are released into the new plant. As the temperatures fall towards their winter levels we now find plants (whether grown from seeds, corms or cormlets) which have made leaf growth, and are now capable of initiating flower buds. This they do as the temperatures drop further, and then the buds develop to give a flowering plant in the winter, the point at which we joined the cycle.

When we come to look at the cultural requirements for growing freesias commercially, many of the factors we have to consider will be found to relate directly to the natural life cycle of the plant. To give one or two examples, the corm, after lifting at the end of the crop, will need to be given a three month period of heat treatment at 30°C before it is replanted. This treatment is necessary to break the dormancy of the corm and to allow active growth to begin when the temperature drops at planting time. Without this artificial 'South African summer' corms will generally remain inactive, and will eventually begin to sprout slowly and irregularly. Before this fact was realised, freesia corms were described as having a tendency to 'sleep' every second year, and so reliable production of plants from corms was limited to stock imported to Europe from South Africa after natural heat treatment had been given, and planted directly on delivery.

A second, and particularly important, example relates to flower initiation. The freesia plant, as will be described in more detail later, becomes able to initiate flower buds after it has reached a particular stage in its vegetative growth. At this time the cultural conditions which are given are critical, particularly as far as temperature is concerned, as this will determine to a large extent all the factors which are of importance to the commercial grower – the number of stems produced, the length of the stems, the number of buds per stem, and the proportion and type of flower deformities. The optimum conditions will be seen to be quite similar to the natural climatic conditions which a plant in the wild would receive during the autumn months. Overall temperatures should be quite cool; a mean soil temperature at corm depth of below 18°C is suitable. A falling temperature regime gives a better crop than a static or increasing one, and there should be no widely fluctuating temperatures, particularly between day and night.

Other examples of the significance of the biology and natural history of the freesia plant to commercial practices will become obvious as cultural aspects of freesia growing are considered, including seed treatment to get good germination, suitable conditions for good corm multiplication rates, and the various corm treatments available for extending or varying the cropping programme. Most of these cultural requirements have been elucidated in the last twenty five years, some by growers' trial and error, others by experimentation or research, and still others by direct consideration of the life cycle of the freesia in is natural habitat. The outcome is that the commercial freesia grower is now equipped with a sound physiological basis for his cultural techniques. While occasional faults or even crop failures may still occur, they will now be explicable in terms of faults in culture, and a reliable and profitable growing programme can be developed by the intelligent grower.

FIG 2
A well-grown crop of named-variety freesias in bud. Such a crop will produce very uniform blooms, and the main stems will be cut over a period of as little as seven to ten days.

Structure and development

Finally, at this stage, a little needs to be said about the structure and development of the freesia plant, so that later references will be more easily visualised by the reader. If we start with a germinating seed, we find that the young plant first builds up a leaf and root system. The root system of a freesia plant is quite fibrous, and the majority of the active root lies in the top 20cm of the soil. In addition to this fibrous root system there develop one or more large fleshy, contractile roots. These roots are capable of adjusting the depth of the plant in the soil, so that a corm which is planted too deep or too shallow will tend to find its own optimum depth.

The leaves of the freesia plant are initiated from the single growing point in succession, in two alternate rows, so that the plant appears to be flattened in one plane. The diagrammatic view in figure two can be compared with the actual appearance of the plant alongside. During the early vegetative phase of the plant, leaves are initiated and developed in sequence until the point at which the plant becomes capable of flower bud initiation. This point depends on the variety or strain, and on whether the plant has grown from seed, corm or cormlet, but is usually within the range 6-9 leaves. From this time onwards the

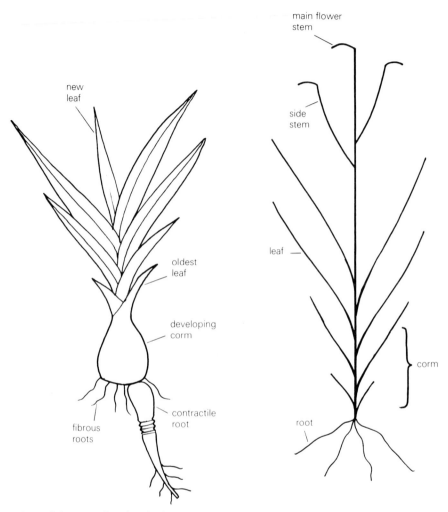

Figure 2 Structure of the freesia plant

plant is able to initiate its flower buds instead of a further leaf. When this happens no further leaves are initiated, as the flower stem terminates the development of the aerial part of the plant.

It is important to note that the process of flower initiation does not automatically take place as soon as the plant has reached this stage. Initiation is dependent on the climate, especially the temperature, and if this is not suitable the plant will continue to produce leaves until the right conditions do occur. If such conditions are considerably delayed, then as many as twenty leaves may

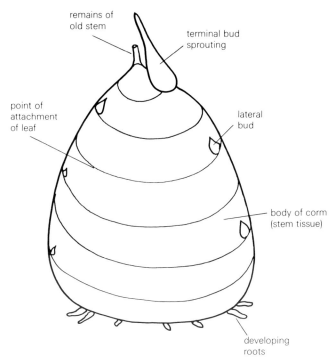

Figure 3 Freesia corm at planting time (tunic removed)

be produced, and flowering is greatly retarded. Eventually, however, flower initiation will take place, and at that time the structure of the flower stem, the number and position of side-break stems (representing the yield to the commercial grower) and the number of buds on each stem are all determined. This emphasises once more the importance of this phase of growth in commercial crops.

At the same time that the aerial part of the plant is developing towards maturity, the plant is producing a new corm at its base. This becomes fully formed and mature soon after flowering, at which time the foliage starts to die back. Structurally, the body of the corm consists of the swollen base of the stem (figure three), containing nutrients which will be assimilated during the early growth of the corm the following year. The outer tunic of the corm, which has the appearance of several papery layers, is formed from the dried off bases of the leaves. These are attached at different levels on the corm, and at each point of attachment there is a single bud. Morphologically, this is the axillary bud of the leaf with which it is associated, and, because of the bilateral symmetry of the plant, these buds form two opposite rows down the corm.

In addition to the corm, there may be formed one or more cormlets at its base. These develop from the lower axillary buds, and provide a secondary source of stored food material. Cormlets do not generally start to form until the plant is in flower, but reach maturity at the same time as the main corm. Together with the axillary buds on the corm, these cormlets represent the plant's potential for vegetative multiplication, an important factor when commercial corm stocks have to be bulked up. As described above, only a single new plant usually develops from a corm, as the remaining axillary buds are inhibited by the developing terminal bud. The cormlets, however, become quite separated from the parent corm, and are therefore not subject to this inhibition. Each produces a new plant capable of flowering in its first season. Because of this, it is possible to produce a higher multiplication rate for a stock of corms by providing the optimum cultural conditions for cormlet production, and then by encouraging extra shoot development on the parent corm. This can be done by removing or killing the terminal bud, and so allowing the axillary buds to grow.

2: General Culture

Before embarking on the commercial production of cut-flower freesias it is necessary to consider the cultural requirements for the crop, and to examine how they may best be achieved. Climatic considerations are of great importance, since the type of equipment needed will depend on how far one has to depart from the natural climate of the area, and also on how far one wishes to depart from the natural growing season of the freesia in order to programme production for particular market requirements. To take extreme examples, a grower in South Africa who wishes to produce freesia flowers for sale in the winter months can do so with great ease, whereas a grower situated in the Mediterranean region aiming to flower a crop in late summer will do so only with difficulty. He will have to employ techniques which allow bud initiation to take place under climatically adverse conditions.

The recommendations set out here refer principally to the temperate climate regions of Western Europe. Even within this region there will be temperature variations from area to area, particularly in the severity of the winter and in the mean summer temperatures. This must be borne in mind when interpreting the notes that follow, and growers in areas far removed from this temperate region will need to refer to the chapters devoted to particular cultural programmes to consider how the temperature requirements of these programmes may best be achieved in their own situation.

Structures

It will be assumed that the grower wishes to produce his crops under protected cultivation. This will not always be the case as it may be that, as in South Africa, the climate will allow natural season production outdoors. For example, until the last few years Guernsey freesia growers traditionally sowed seed outdoors in pots in the early spring, and these plants remained outside until buds were visible in the autumn, when they were moved into glasshouses for cropping to avoid spoiling the bloom in the wet, windy conditions which often occur at that time. By growing a slightly earlier crop, or giving some protection from the worst of the weather, it would be possible to grow the entire crop outdoors.

FIG 3
Mobile structures can be very suitable for freesia growing in temperate climates. One crop can be started into growth under cover, and then grown without protection until cropping commences. The structure can also be used to provide shading if conditions warrant this.

However, whatever the climate of the area under consideration, outdoor cropping will allow only a very limited production period, and with the emphasis now placed by markets on year-round supply there is always pressure to programme crops to flower outside their natural season. To do this requires a structure of some type, either glass or polythene-covered, and may require little or much ventilation according to local conditions. Whether or not a heating system is required will also depend on the climate. To answer these questions, we must look at the temperature and other needs of the freesia crop, and the grower will then be able to see what type of structure and equipment is necessary for his own production programme.

To provide complete freedom of programming around the year it is necessary to be able to control soil temperature, at a depth of 8 centimetres, within the range 10-15°C during the winter months, and 15-20°C in the summer. Less control than this will reduce the flexibility of crop timing, but not necessarily to the extent that freesia growing becomes impractical.

Assuming that the grower is using a glasshouse for freesia production, we can now consider the particular equipment which should be installed. The glasshouse iself should provide reasonable light transmission. Although freesias are less sensitive to low light levels than many other crops it is still necessary to maintain adequate light if it is intended to produce a crop through the winter

FIG 4
If crops are to be started outside, and then housed for flowering, a suitable standing-out ground is necessary. This should be covered with gravel over polythene for weed control and drainage, and shaded to prevent the sun from falling directly onto the pots.

months. Older structures, apart from problems of ventilation and working height, are less suitable for winter and early spring production, encouraging lower yields and generally poor quality blooms.

Ventilation must be considered as a major factor. Even if it is not intended to crop through the peak temperatures of the summer months it will still be necessary to provide good ventilation to cut down excessive day temperatures in spring and autumn. A high day-night temperature differential leads to serious flower abnormalities if it occurs during the bud initiation period, and cooling by overhead sprays and shading must be thought of as only secondary to good ventilation. As far as possible, ventilators should be arranged to avoid the sun falling directly onto the soil, as this leads to localised high temperature spots and to excessive drying out of the soil. Side ventilators are a worthwhile addition to those in the roof of the structure, particularly in areas where high summer temperatures are not reliably moderated by cooling winds.

Polythene tunnels can be used successfully for freesia growing, but have limitations. The greatest problem is that of humidity. The freesia is very sensitive to botrytis bloom spotting, and this fungal disease develops rapidly under high humidity conditions. Polythene tunnels are therefore most useful where the crop is flowering under low humidity conditions, or where a particularly good ventilation system has been installed. The ability to introduce heat into the crop through low-level pipes is of great value in the prevention or control of botrytis, and a heating system of this type greatly increases the flexibility of freesia growing in polythene-clad structures. Tunnels have one major advantage over static glasshouses. The cladding material can easily be removed during the summer months, making it possible to reduce soil temperatures down to the levels at which flower bud initiation can take place. This advantage can be taken one stage further, and the cladding can be replaced with a woven plastic material which will shade the soil while still allowing enough air movement for evaporative cooling of the crop.

One type of structure which can be used to good effect for freesia growing is the mobile glasshouse. A highly flexible system is possible using such houses, with the crop being covered as necessary for seed germination, early growth of corms, and the cropping period, and uncovered for the critical bud initiation stage. Other types of protected cultivation can be used for freesias according to climatic conditions and the degree of flexibility of cropping programme needed.

Heating system

Whether a heating system is to be installed will depend on a number of factors. As we have already discussed, some areas of production will be able to grow freesias for particular seasons by relying solely on the natural climatic cycle. In other situations considerable heat input to the crop will be necessary. The sort of temperature range which will give the most flexibility of cropping — 10-20°C in the upper soil layer according to season — should indicate whether a heating system is necessary in a particular area. It must also be remembered, however, that the ability to introduce heat into a freesia crop when it is at the flowering stage can be of value in reducing humidity, and therefore in preventing botrytis, even if the temperature range would be satisfactory without this. Similarly, as we will see later, the application of a little heat together with some ventilation is important under some conditions to maintain active plant growth by keeping a buoyant atmosphere around the crop.

As far as the type of heating system is concerned, the principal alternatives are warm air heating, large or small bore pipes above ground, and under-soil heating. Of these, warm air heating is generally the least suitable. This is because there are likely to be occasions when a steady application of a low heat level is wanted to maintain a drying air flow through the crop, whereas warm air systems are more effective when being used to apply intermittent bursts of heat. Pipe systems are better, and for the same reason it is preferable to use larger diameter pipes which can operate at low water temperatures rather than small bore steam or pressurised hot water systems. The pipes should be distributed close to ground level and within the crop, rather than above the crop or around the perimeter of the glasshouse, for maximum usefulness.

It has already been mentioned that for the period of bud initiation it is the soil temperature which is critical. For this reason alone there is a worth-while advantage in under-soil heating. There are also other advantages to such a system, which have resulted in many freesia growers installing sub-soil heating units. To maintain active plant growth during the winter months the soil temperature is more important than the air temperature, and in fact a soil temperature two or three degrees higher than the air temperature is frequently recommended. This differential in turn stimulates air movement through the foliage, keeping the crop dry and disease free. Additionally, under-soil heating is significantly more economical to run where air temperatures can be kept quite low, and this in iself may be enough to justify such an installation in situations where a high winter fuel requirement is a problem. Finally, an under-soil heating system of the standard type — such as plastic pipe loops buried to a depth of 45-50cm — can also be employed in the summer for soil cooling if a refrigeration unit is added to the system.

Irrigation systems

According to the conditions and season in which they are grown, freesias may need to be watered as often as daily or as seldom as once in three or four weeks. There are several methods of applying water, most of which are suitable provided their limitations are understood. During the early stages of growth, when there is little foliage, either low-level or overhead spraylines can be used. Unless the planting density is very low, low-level systems are less satisfactory when the crop is more advanced, because of the difficulty of getting spread of water to the edges of the beds. Because of this, the most common irrigation systems used by freesia growers are forms of overhead sprinklers or spraylines. A coarse, heavy spray gives the best distribution for the lowest installation cost, but fine misting nozzles have the advantage that they can also be used for crop cooling during the summer. One disadvantage of overhead systems is that they can cause cultural problems, particularly in crops flowering in the winter, by encouraging the spread of disease through the crop while the foliage is wet, but this effect can be reduced by applying water less frequently, and early in the day during bright weather.

Other watering methods, notably trickle or drip irrigation systems, can be used, provided they are able to give a uniform application of water across the full width of the bed. In these days of automation it may seem archaic to even mention the hose. However, for small areas of production, especially where

FIG 5
Adequate crop supports are important to keep the foliage upright. They do not need to be expensive – in Guernsey it is standard to use old greenhouse timber to support layers of galvanised wire mesh. The layers are moved up with the crop as it grows.

heavy soils allow watering frequency to be reduced, hose watering is quite adequate, and in the hands of an intelligent grower can give a distribution of water as close to the optimum as any automatic installation. Whatever system is adopted, a hose should still be available, and used at regular intervals to maintain uniformity of watering over the crop.

Although freesias are rather insensitive to fertiliser levels in the soil, there will be occasions when the application of nutrients to a crop is called for. Although this can be done by using granular fertiliser dressings, it is better to use liquid fertilisers, and so the irrigation system installed should make provision for this. A number of proprietary dilution systems are available for this purpose, and all are equally suitable provided they offer reasonable accuracy. Alternatively, if the watering system works from a storage tank or cistern then the appropriate quantity of liquid fertiliser can be diluted directly into the full volume of water. In this way, the accuracy of the dilute feed solution applied to the crop is certain.

FIG 6
Inadequate crop supports can cause serious cultural problems later in the life of the crop. The foliage layers down, and high moisture levels under the leaves encourage botrytis and bacterial rots. Once the crop has got into this condition, corrective measures are almost impossible.

Crop cooling

The extent to which soil temperatures can be kept down to acceptable levels is the greatest single factor in determining how flexible a freesia growing programme can be. The importance of temperature control, and particularly of avoiding large fluctuations in the temperature, cannot be over emphasised in relation to the flower initiation stage of growth. Avoiding low temperatures is a relatively simple matter, but there are a number of alternative ways of reducing high soil temperatures; and combinations of any of these may be necessary according to local conditions.

Ventilation systems have already been discussed, but when considering the equipment needed for growing freesias the year round it is necessary to think also in terms of overhead spraying or misting units in most growing areas. To make full use of the air flow produced by a good ventilation system, the crop and soil should be regularly damped down during hot weather, so that evaporative cooling can produce a temperature drop. The simplest way of doing this is to install an overhead watering system, and to turn this on for a few seconds at intervals through the day, bearing in mind that the total volume of water that reaches the soil should not exceed the requirements of the crop. At the other extreme, a fully automated misting system, perhaps programmed to operate with an electronic 'leaf' sensing device, will give optimum cooling conditions. According to local humidity conditions, 'fan and pad' installations may be an effective way of cooling. In this sytem, ventilation of the structure is by means of fans, and air is drawn into the house through pads of porous material, through which water is trickled, thus giving an evaporative cooling effect at the time that air enters the structure rather than within the crop.

Various forms of crop shading may also be of value for cooling the soil during the summer months. This can range from simply putting lime onto the outside of the structure, or applying a proprietary material which changes its opacity according to humidity conditions, to various shading materials supported above the crop. There is no problem of light requirement in the summer with freesias, and so liming can be successfully used provided it is removed before light levels fall towards autumn levels. In the case of shading materials such as hessian or woven plastic sheeting care must be taken in the layout to avoid trapping warm air beneath the shade, and thus aggravating rather than improving the situation.

Another cooling method which may be considered according to local conditions is mulching the soil with a light-reflecting material such as Styromull. This is of little value once the crop has developed a good foliage height, but will help to avoid high soil temperatures building up during the early stages of growth. At the other extreme of cost is the provisions of a refrigeration unit attached to under-soil plastic pipes, which can then circulate cooled water. This is an expensive operation both for installation and in running costs, but is considered an economic proposition by several Dutch freesia growers, who can greatly improve the reliability of their cropping programme by providing a soil cooling facility of as little as three or four degrees centigrade.

Crop support

A system of crop supports is necessary for freesias, because, although the crop is a short-term one and the leaf height rarely exceeds one metre, the foliage is soft, and would fall over without support. This in turn would give a number of cultural problems, particularly in relation to the spread of diseases in the damp conditions under the leaf canopy. The supports do not need to be structurally massive or elaborate, but must have sufficient layers to hold up leaves of varying height – this may require only a single layer in the case of some quick-producing corm crops, or up to three layers if the crop is leafy and slow to flower. In both Holland and Guernsey it is standard to use galvanised wire netting with a mesh size of 13cm square. This is available in widths to fit commonly used bed sizes, and can easily be lifted, cleaned and rolled up ready for re-use on the following crop. Where this cannot be obtained any similar netting would be suitable, or alternatively a plastic, cotton or string system which could be disposed of after cropping.

Other equipment

Growers in the main areas of production usually rely on specialists who provide a service for heat treatment of freesia corms. Those who do not have access to such a service, or perhaps prefer to have the extra flexibility which their own corm treatment unit can provide, will need to build or adapt a suitable structure. According to the size of the production unit, the store may need to be large or small, but the climatic requirements in either case are the same. The basic heat treatment of corms needs a temperature of 30°C, and this needs to be controlled within two or three degrees either way. In addition, it is often an advantage to have a holding store which can be run at around 10-14°C. This can be used either for corms or for cut flowers.

The actual treatment requirements will depend on the growing programme, and aspects of this will be considered in detail in chapter four. For example, humidity control may also be necessary according to the natural humidity levels of the region. If it is intended to attempt the early flowering treatment of freesia corms described later, then a more elaborate store will be needed, with precise temperature and humidity control and fans to provide air movement within the unit.

Enriching the atmosphere of the glasshouse with carbon dioxide is a common technique in commercial horticulture, and the freesia grower will need to consider whether to invest in equipment for this purpose. Unfortunately, there is no experimental evidence which clearly defines the economics of carbon dioxide enrichment on freesias. Because the freesia plant has a lower temperature requirement than many crops, it is reasonable to assume from first principles that any advantage from more than ambient levels of carbon dioxide will be less than in crops grown at higher temperatures. So, it is unlikely that installing equipment for this purpose is a sound economic proposition, in view of the running costs of enrichment. An exception may be where exhaust boiler gases from the combustion of natural gas can be fed into the glasshouse, as is the practice in Holland. However, this must not be attempted unless it is known that these exhaust gases are free of the noxious products which normally accompany combustion, otherwise severe crop damage can occur.

Seed or corms?

To conclude this chapter on the equipment and materials needed for freesia growing we must now consider the type of planting material which is to be used. While a discussion on the most suitable varieties to grow will be left until the appropriate chapter on cultural aspects of the crop, the first decision which has to be made is whether to grow a crop from seed or from corms. This decision may have to be made on the grounds of availability, but on the assumption that suitable varieties of both seed and corms are available (as they generally are in the main centres of freesia production), there are a number of other factors which have to be taken into account.

The most important difference between seed and corm crops is the time during which the crop occupies the glasshouse. In the case of seed-grown freesias the crop generally needs about ten to twelve months, depending on the sowing date and the temperature regime. Corm crops can be expected to be in the ground for only seven to ten months under equivalent conditions – or even less for named variety corms, which tend to flower more uniformly over a shorter period. This means that some cropping schedules will require corm crops if the programme is to work, while others will be more suited to seed crops. The actual period of flowering is more extended for seed crops, too, and this can be an advantage where heavy labour peaks need to be avoided during the picking and marketing period. On the other hand, a short, heavy crop may be more suitable if the crop is to be timed to bulk for a particular demand period.

The other main consideration when choosing between seed and corms is the problem of disease transfer. A stock of corms may always harbour a small proportion of disease – virus, fusarium or bacterial rot – which may not be noticed at planting time. In the case of fusarium in particular this can lead to contamination of previously disease-free soil with a problem which is then difficult to eradicate. Even where the stock of corms has previously been grown on the property rather than purchased there is the possibility that disease had become established in the crop during the final weeks before lifting, and not noticed at that time. Seed, however, is not known to transfer any of the diseases which affect freesias, and so a crop grown from seed sown in clean soil should remain clean. On the other hand, seedlings of freesias grow slowly in the early stages, and are particularly susceptible to fusarium infection at that time, so they are less suitable for soils where there is a risk of this disease already being present.

Other factors will come to light during consideration of the cultural requirements for the two types of crop, such as the need to use corms if one wishes to grow high-uniformity blooms or double-flowered varieties, or the need to grow from seed to provide clean corms to replace older, diseased stocks.

3: Growing from Seed

Freesias can be grown either from seed or from corms, and in each case will flower in their first year. In Guernsey, seed crops have always been an important part of the freesia industry. At one time they represented at least three quarters of the total area of freesias, being mainly sown outdoors in the early spring and housed for autumn flowering. More recently, there has been a considerable swing towards crops grown by specialists using year-round programmes. This has brought about a reduction in the proportion of freesias grown from seed. However, seed crops still occupy around thirty acres of glass in the Island, and produce twenty five million blooms annually.

Seed strains

There are a number of different strains of seed available commercially. With one or two minor exceptions, these strains are high quality tetraploids (see chapter one), and are all suitable for cut flower production at any time of the year. Whenever these strains have been examined experimentally it has usually been found that there are only small yield differences between them, and that the lower yielding strains tend to give slightly better quality. This being the case, financial returns vary little between strains, and the choice becomes one of personal preference or availability.

Some strains, particularly the new introductions, are available as separate colours — red, pink, blue, yellow and white. Within each colour there is generally a range of shades and flower shape. This lack of uniformity means that the market will not generally want bunches of a single colour. Despite this, it is worth considering growing freesias in beds of separate colours, even where a mixed bunch is to be marketed. This is because the strength and height of the foliage varies from colour to colour, and so the weaker-growing colours tend to be swamped when grown in a mixed colour bed. There is often some difference in timing between colours, and where this is known for a particular strain the quickest flowering colour can be the last sown, so making the marketing of mixed bunches rather easier.

Soil preparation

Freesias are tolerant of a wide range of soil types, and can be grown successfully in most horticultural regions provided the cultural techniques used (watering and feeding) are appropriate to the soil. When preparing new sites for freesia cultivation, attention must be paid in particular to soil structure and drainage, as the soil is often compacted. Good drainage and aeration are important, as the strength of the side-stems, and hence the marketable yield, depends on a good root system. The roots of the freesia plant are fibrous, and do not require a great depth of soil. Twenty centimetres (8in) is enough, provided the soil moisture content can be kept at the right level. There is one apparent exception to the freesia's tolerance of substrates, and that is in the case of peat. Freesias are very susceptible to leaf scorch caused by fluoride toxicity (see chapter five), and this symptom is commonly induced in peat substrates or soils with a high peat content. This is because these substrates tend to have a low pH and low available calcium, and both these factors aggravate the symptom of fluoride damage. For this reason, peat dressings added for soil conditioning should not be used in excessive amounts.

As far as the nutrient status of the soil is concerned, the lime content should be rather high, again to reduce the risk of fluoride leaf scorch occurring, and a pH of 6.5 or higher should be the aim. Freesias have been shown to be quite insensitive to the levels of the major nutrients in the soil, very little effect being produced through a wide range. Because of this it is better to use no base fertiliser dressings at all unless soil analysis indicates a clear deficiency. Excess nutrients, causing high salt levels in the soil, result in root scorch and stunted growth in the crop, particularly if the soil is allowed to dry back at any time. This risk is increased if unnecessary base fertilisers are used. High nitrogen levels produce their own problems, encouraging flower distortion and also giving a banded effect on the flower stem caused by excessive vegetative growth. Phosphate fertilisers should also be used with caution, as many commercially-used phosphate sources contain fluoride as a contaminant, so adding to the risk of fluoride toxicity symptoms.

The soil sterilisation programme adopted before sowing freesia seed will depend on a number of factors, including the disease and weed status of previous crops, and is discussed at greater length in chapter five. It is important to bear in mind that seed freesias occupy the glasshouse for a longer time than corms, and for much of that time are small plants, susceptible to soil-borne disease and to being swamped by weed growth. Because of this, soil sterilisation should be particularly thorough for freesia crops grown from seed.

FIG 7
Commercial seed production is carried out in large blocks using bees for pollination. Each colour group
is grown in a separate area to prevent 'muddy' colours which result from cross-pollinating between two
different colours.

Seed treatment

Tetraploid freesia seed is rather slow and erratic to germinate because it has a
hard, impermeable seed coat. Treatment of the seed before sowing can reduce
this problem and allow rapid, uniform germination, provided suitable cultural
conditions are given after sowing. Treatment should consist of two stages.
Firstly, the seed should be scarified. This means that the hard seed coat should
be chipped and partially removed. This is achieved by rubbing the seed between
two sheets of sandpaper, or between a single sheet of sandpaper and a hard
surface. Growers doing this for the first time may be understandably nervous
because of the risk of damage to expensive seed, but no harm will be done if
scarifying is continued until a significant amount of dusty seed-coat chipping
has been produced.

After scarifying, the seed should be soaked for about twenty four hours in
water at room temperature. This allows the process of water uptake to begin.

The length of soaking is not critical, although seed should be treated in small enough batches so that it can be sown quite soon after soaking. It is possible that the soaking treatment also removes a water-soluble inhibitory chemical from the seed-coat, which otherwise retards germination. On the assumption that this may be the case, it may be worthwhile discarding and replacing the water once or twice during the soaking period. At the end of this period the seed should be lightly dried to prevent it from sticking together and so make handling easier for sowing. This can be done by spreading the seed out on newspaper or blotting paper, and can be accelerated if necessary by playing over gently with hand-held hair dryer. Care must be taken not to allow localised over-heating which could damage the seed. Sowing should follow within twenty four hours of drying off the seed.

Seed sowing

It has been suggested in the past that freesia seed can be chitted in peat, or on moist paper, and then sown as emergence occurs. However, the seedlings suffer a considerable check when this is done, and so this method is no longer generally recommended. Where chitting is carried out, a seedling with a more fibrous root system, which is better able to withstand transplanting, is obtained if germination temperatures are on the high side.

Where seed is to be sown direct in the glasshouse soil, it should be placed at a maximum depth of a quarter of an inch, so that it is just covered. Freesia seed germinates better in darkness than in light, and so this covering is important. The sowing density should make allowance for some germination failure — good cultural conditions will give a germination level of about 85-90%. The plants from seed strains should generally be spaced at about 12-14 per square foot (125-150 per square metre), and so a seed sowing at 3ins square will give the right final plant density. Slightly higher densities may be satisfactory for crops growing through the spring and flowering in summer and early autumn, but crops grown for winter and early spring production should be at rather lower density to prevent disease problems. Where seed batches of separate colours are being sown, this should be in proportion to the colour balance required for marketing — a suitable balance is usually obtained with 30% yellow, 20% each red, pink and blue, and 10% white. To estimate the weight of seed required, it should be assumed that mixed colour tetraploids have 1,600-1,800 seeds per ounce (55-65 per gram), according to variety. Older strains, especially diploids, were smaller-seeded, and contained up to 3,000 seeds per ounce (105 per gram).

There are various devices which can assist in the rather tedious job of seed

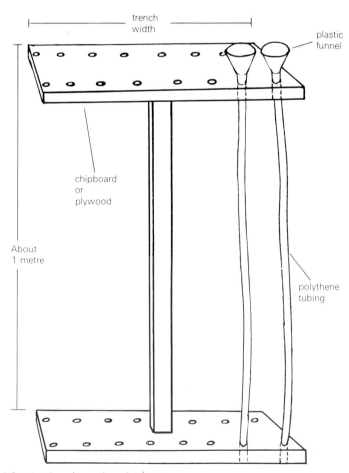

Figure 4 Construction of a seed-sowing frame.

sowing. The simplest, which can be made by the grower and which allows sowing to be carried out in the standing position, consists of two boards of plywood or similar, each drilled with holes to take polythene tubing (see diagram), through which the seed can be dropped via small plastic funnels. There are also more complicated devices available, such as those in which the seeds are picked up by a fan-produced vacuum and released on to the soil surface when the vacuum is broken. Fully mechanical seed sowing as is available for agriculture has not yet been developed for freesias, but the possibility of using a tractor-driven fluid drilling machine for freesias is at present under investigation in England.

FIG 8
Faulty germination of seed is generally the result of wrong temperatures — either too high or too low —
or of insufficient moisture in the upper layers of the soil.

Seed germination

The temperature and soil moisture conditions needed for germination of freesia seed are quite critical and many cases of poor and erratic emergence can be traced back to unsatisfactory culture. Freesia seed requires a fairly high temperature for good germination — 18 to 22°C is suitable. Temperatures below 15°C will greatly retard emergence, and the final crop stand may also be reduced. Similarly, germination failure often follows excessively high soil temperatures caused by direct sun heat, and this should be avoided by shading summer sowings.

Soil moisture levels are also important, particularly as the seed is close to the surface where drying out is most likely. It is essential to keep the soil to this depth uniformly moist, without waterlogging, until emergence is complete. Any dry patches, even for a short time, will result in slow and erratic emergence. To help in maintaining suitable moisture levels it is possible to cover the surface of the bed with hessian or other suitable material to reduce evaporation. This will also help by reducing temperature fluctuations.

Pre-germination of seed

It is possible to raise freesia seedlings in paper or peat squares in seedling boxes for planting out after emergence. This is a valuable technique if it would be difficult or expensive to provide suitable germination conditions in the glasshouse, as the boxes can be close spaced into a much smaller area. It is also useful if the cropping programme is tight, as it allows the first month or so of the crop to take place outside the glasshouse which will eventually be used for cropping. Although there are additional costs involved, these are often justified because of the above advantages, and also because the ability to apply more precise temperature and moisture control to the boxes will result in a higher germination percentage.

The technique is a simple one. Seedling boxes of any type are filled with small propagation units made either of compressed peat (such as 1¼ inch squares) or of paper, and these are loosely filled with a peat-based propagation compost. This is lightly pressed down to leave a quarter of an inch of pot visible. Seed is then sown in the pots — usually three or four per pot according to size of container — and covered with a little compost. The boxes are watered, and can then be stacked until emergence begins, after which they are spaced out on to benches or on the floor. The pots should be planted out about 7-14 days after emergence, which means about 3-5 weeks after sowing according to temperature. Pot spacing in the bed will obviously depend on the number of seeds sown per pot and on the required final plant density in the house.

When planting out seedlings in this way it is important that the top edge of the pot should not stick out above the soil level, particularly in the case of compressed peat pots. The pot will dry out excessively if this happens, and will become a barrier to the rooting out of the seedlings into the bed. Slow establishment of the young plants into the bed will result in a poor crop with stunted foliage, and so rapid rooting out should be encouraged by maintaining a suitable temperature — shading from the sun in summer, or applying heat in the winter — and spraying over occasionally to maintain humidity and to keep the upper layers of the soil moist.

Early growth

Until the bud initiation stage, freesia seedlings will grow satisfactorily over quite a wide temperature range, although extremes should be avoided. During the winter, 10°C will ensure continued but slow growth, while 12-15°C will allow more rapid plant development if this is important for crop timing. It must be remembered that the higher the winter temperature, then the more important becomes light transmission if weak, drawn plants are to be avoided. It may be preferable to run a day temperature a little higher than the night temperature, but it is unlikely that this is of great importance, especially as any sun heat will produce such a differential naturally. In the summer, soil temperatures may be allowed to rise to 25°C without harm, but under such conditions the crop should be regularly damped over to maintain air humidity and thus enable the plant to continue to grow actively. However, since lower soil temperatures will be needed subsequently for bud initiation it is wise to anticipate this by using the various techniques described in chapter two to reduce high soil temperatures during this period of early growth.

Watering freesia seedlings is a simple matter, even though the quantities and frequency of application will vary enormously according to the season. As with temperatures, it is only a question of avoiding extremes, although in the case of watering some fluctuation is a definite advantage. Continuously moist soil encourages a rather small root system on the plants, as they have no incentive to search for water. This may cause problems during the later stages if conditions of stress then occur. Because of this, it is better to allow a little drying back between waterings once the young plants are well established, so developing a deeper root system. The exception to this is where high salt levels occur in the soil for any reason, and in this situation drying back will cause loss of root by scorching, and should be avoided.

As already indicated, freesias have a low requirement for soil nutrients, and the feeding programme is therefore quite flexible. It is usual to apply the first liquid feed to a seed crop at about the time when flower bud initiation begins, and to repeat this four to six weeks later. Depending on the soil type it is unlikely that any further feeding will be necessary after this. The type of feed used will depend mainly on the season. To encourage softer growth for the summer months it is usual to feed during the spring with a medium nitrogen feed, while, conversely, autumn feeding should be with a medium potash feed to harden the growth for the winter. A high nitrogen feed should only be used when it is necessary to encourage the development of stronger growth, and should be avoided under normal conditions. The formulae and recommendations for making up these various types of feed will be found at the end of this book.

As the crop grows, it will be necessary to either add or raise the crop supports, according to the type used. Where wire mesh is used, it is best to sow or plant out the crop through the layers, which have previously been placed on the soil. In this way, the mesh can be used as a guide for plant spacing, and the plants remain neatly supported, as the layers are gradually raised with growth. Until the time when temperature control becomes more important for flower bud initiation, there is little else which demands consideration in the way of routine crop management, except that a regular inspection should be made for pest and disease problems. These are described, and appropriate prevention or control measures noted, in a later chapter. This aspect of freesia culture should not be disregarded just because the crop appears at this stage to need no attention. Rather, the low labour requirement for routine work should enable the grower to apply extra time to the prevention of pests or diseases at this stage. These can otherwise become quickly established in the crop and cause losses

FIG 9
Seed can be pre-germinated in peat squares in
boxes. Suitable conditions for rapid and uniform
emergence can be given more accurately, and
more economically, than if the seed is direct
sown.

FIG 10
Seed sown in peat squares should be encouraged
to root out quickly into the border soil after
planting. The soil should remain moist until this is
achieved. Note the three layers of nets already in
position to be raised as the crop grows.

out of all proportion to the effort which would have been needed to prevent
them.

At this time, too, it may be an advantage to clip over the foliage to reduce the
height, although this is more usually done rather later, when leaf extension
growth is nearly finished. However, the later it is left, the greater the risk of
cutting through early buds which have elongated inside the leaf sheath. Cutting
down the foliage is by no means a necessary cultural technique in most crops,
but it is sometimes convenient where leaf height is excessive, to avoid later
problems with picking and with disease control. The crops which are most likely
to benefit from cutting over are those initiating bud rather late; that is, during the
summer months. In some crops, cutting over may be carried out twice, or even
three times, apparently without detriment to either yield or quality.

Bud initiation

The importance of the bud initiation stage of growth has already been
mentioned, but must again be emphasised. During this short period in the life
cycle of the plants — only a few days if conditions are right — are determined,
more or less irreversibly, both the yield and the quality of the crop. It is obviously
important for the grower to know when this stage has been reached. In the case
of a crop grown from seed the exact time will vary from plant to plant, and so it is
necessary to provide suitable bud initiation conditions over quite a long period
of time. This is because variations occur in the speed of germination and
emergence of the seedlings, and also in the subsequent growth rate of the

young plants. In the case of corms, and in particular named variety corms, the uniformity of growth rate is much greater, and so the bud initiation stage of a commercial crop is shorter.

For a seed-grown crop, it should be assumed that the bud initiation stage commences when the majority of the crop has the fifth leaf visible, and continues for six weeks if soil temperatures average less than 15°C, or longer if temperatures are higher than this. In summer conditions there can be considerable delays to initiation, and therefore to flowering, if soil temperatures remain high. Flowering can be set back three months or more if summer temperatures are high, and there is a proportional increase in the number and height of the leaves when this happens.

Of the various cultural conditions which can affect a crop, only one, temperature, is of importance in determining bud initiation factors. In particular, it is the temperature in the soil at corm depth which matters, and a thermometer pushed into the soil to this depth is an absolute essential at this stage. As a general rule, and where accurate temperature control is not possible, a temperature averaging 13-17°C throughout the initiation period will give a satisfactory yield, and provided excessive fluctuations are avoided, such as are caused by sun heat on the soil, the bloom quality should also be reasonable. The greatest danger is in spring and autumn, when cold nights and sunny days give a high temperature differential, and flower deformities result. An average temperature below 13°C will give premature bud initiation, and cause the crop to flower early on short foliage. This results in a low yield of short, poor quality stems. A mean temperature of 17°C or above will delay flowering, but the yield and quality should still be satisfactory.

Where accurate temperature control is possible, then the temperature regime during bud initiation can be planned to provide optimum conditions for a good yield and flower quality. For example, the yield will be maximum at a mean temperature of about 13°C, since this is the temperature at which most side-breaks are initiated. The yield is generally better if there is a falling temperature regime over the initiation period, rather than a constant or increasing regime. Stem length, on the other hand, is greatest with an average temperature of 18°C or above, high day temperatures being particularly important. There are other conflicting factors — the high day temperatures needed for good stem length will also increase the proportion of distorted blooms if the night temperatures are low, and if they are not then flowering will be delayed and yield reduced. The number of florets on each stem also increases with temperature. Corm size and cormlet production further complicate the story. The size of the corms produced increases with temperature, while the number of cormlets, and therefore the multiplication rate of the stock, is greater the lower the temperature. Unlike the flower production effects, however, these corm effects

FIG 11
A typical Guernsey freesia house with pre-germinated seedlings planted out, and the house kept damped down to encourage establishment.

are related to the average temperature throughout the whole growing period, rather than during the bud initiation stage.

Because of these conflicting factors, the temperature regime which will give the optimum crop will depend on the grower's requirements — such as whether his market will pay a premium on quality to compensate for a lower yield, and whether the corm multiplication rate is of importance. The nearest it is possible to get to a standard programme has to make certain assumptions as to which factors are most important. It must also depend on the time of year, as temperatures need to be rather lower during the winter months than in the summer. A compromise programme recommended for the bud initiation stage is as follows:

Summer   Start at 15°C night, 19°C day; reducing gradually to 13°C night, 16°C day.

Winter   Start at 14°C night, 17°C day; reducing gradually to 12°C night, 15°C day.

These are positive temperatures, and a further increase during bright sun is acceptable. If this programme is followed the resulting crop should flower in the minimum time, the yield and stem length should both be not far short of optimum, the number of florets per stem should be satisfactory, and the flowers free of distortion. As already mentioned, it is soil temperature which is the critical factor. Air temperature can be higher or lower without an adverse effect on the cropping potential provided it does not in turn alter the soil temperature unduly.

Later culture

The general culture of seed freesia crops in the later stages is much the same as earlier. Temperatures can be allowed to fluctuate rather more once the bud initiation phase is safely completed. To be sure that this stage is over, it is advisable to dissect several plants by carefully stripping off successive leaves. If bud initiation is complete then it should be possible to see the developing flower stem above the head of the new corm. This will be very small for the first week or two, but reaches 1-2cm after about four weeks. From this stage to flowering will then take a further 8-12 weeks, according to temperature.

Watering and feeding should continue as previously described, although the water requirement of the crop gradually reduces during the picking period. Pest and disease prevention and control measures should be maintained to the end of the crop, particularly where the corms are to be kept. Picking, packing and marketing aspects are covered in chapter six.

Crop clearing

As the picking rates fall below the level at which commercial marketing is practicable, consideration should be given to clearing the crop. If it is not intended to save the stock of corms for future use or for sale, then all that must be done is to dig and discard the plants. It is wise to dig methodically, and to avoid leaving individual corms behind in the bed, as this increases the risk of carry-over of pests or diseases from one crop to the next. This can occur even when no problems have been identified in the growing crop. If the stock of corms is needed, and generally they will be as corms from seed are usually clean, then the plants should not be dug up immediately, but should remain in the soil to mature the corms for a few weeks after flowering. This is not essential, as plants lifted green can be ripened without harm by tying in bundles and hanging in a dry atmosphere until the leaves dry back. The bundles should be small, and the leaves removed as soon as they start to die back, to avoid the risk of spreading botrytis or bacterial soft rot in the stock.

However, although this technique will give sound corms, there will be no production of cormlets, as cormlet development takes place mainly after the completion of flowering. If cormlets are wanted as well as corms the plants must be allowed to ripen off in the soil. At this time, the temperatures may be allowed to fall towards their natural levels if this is in the winter months, and water application can be reduced. In the summer temperatures can be allowed to rise a little. In either case, the soil should never dry back completely, as this encourages soil-borne disease such as fusarium to enter a dormant phase and become much more resistant to control during soil sterilisation. The corm ripening stage may be considered as a part of the corm treatment period, which will be described later. Because of this, the length of heat treatment of corms will vary according to the conditions under which this final stage of growth takes place. If corms ripen in the soil for some time in summer temperatures, then they will subsequently need less than the normal thirteen weeks of treatment to prepare them for active growth, perhaps as little as ten weeks in some circumstances. Conversely, corms dried off in winter soil temperatures may need more time, say 14 or 15 weeks, in heat treatment to complete the breaking of dormancy and to ensure rapid and uniform re-growth when they are planted.

4: Growing from Corms

Freesias grown from corms flower more quickly than those from seed, and generally occupy the glasshouse for only seven to ten months. Flower initiation takes place within the first few weeks after planting or even before planting if the corms are given early-flowering treatment. The crop at that stage is still uniform, and so a temperature programme for optimum cropping is more easily applied than with seed-grown crops.

Choice of stock

One decision which has to be made is whether to use corms produced from a seed crop, or whether to purchase a stock of named variety corms. Corms-from-seed have the main characteristics of seed crops, in that they may be either mixed or single colours, but within each colour there is a range of shades, flower shape, yield and time and flowering. This variability is not necessarily a disadvantage, depending on market requirements, and the longer flowering period of corms-from-seed compared with named variety corms may help even out labour peaks. The yield of corm strains is higher than that of many named variety stocks grown under the same conditions, and the cost of buying in this type of material is much lower. These factors too have to be taken into account, together with an estimate of the market premium which may be obtained from the greater uniformity and quality of named varieties.

Corms from seed may be 'first year' or older. Older stocks of this material produce quite adequate yields, but the risk of fusarium or virus diseases being introduced is greater, and also in mixed stocks there is a tendency for those colours which have a better multiplication rate to build up at the expense of the others, resulting in a poor colour balance.

Named variety corms are technically 'clones', since each variety has been multiplied vegetatively from a single plant. They therefore have the advantage of high uniformity. The yield, timing and quality are easily predictable, according to growing conditions. Some of the new introductions are rather expensive because of the time needed to bulk up stocks once preliminary selection of suitable material has been made, but these newer varieties are generally higher

FIG 12
Corm spacing will depend on the stocks used and on the season. In this case high-value named variety corms have been planted at 13cm square (one per square) to encourage a good rate of corm multiplication, and to make it easier to keep diseases out of the crop.

yielding than older ones. They are also more likely to be disease free. Many older varieties are now difficult to obtain without some virus or leaf necrosis contamination. Once purchased, the high value of named varieties becomes an asset as a good corm multiplication rate will then represent income in the form of sale of surplus stocks. It is common for freesia growers to buy in small numbers of new varieties soon after their introduction, and to grow them in such a way as to encourage a good multiplication rate to build up commercial quantities. If this is done, isolation from the risk of disease infection is obviously very important, and soil sterilisation must be particularly thorough.

The choice of variety will depend to some extent on availability, and also on grower and market preference. No hard and fast rules can be made, particularly with regard to the new varieties which are always being introduced. Yield and quality of named varieties are usually inversely related. For example, the cream double variety Fantasy, which always commands a good market premium, seldom yields two stems per plant, while Rubina, a rather spindly single red, will often provide ten or more cuts at low plant densities, but will sell for a much lower price. The picking and bunching labour required for a crop of Rubina will of course be very much higher than for Fantasy, and this too will contribute to the economics of the choice of variety.

FIG 13
A high plant density is commonly used when growing from cormlets. It is important that such a crop is kept well supported, and the foliage clipped over if it becomes unmanageable.

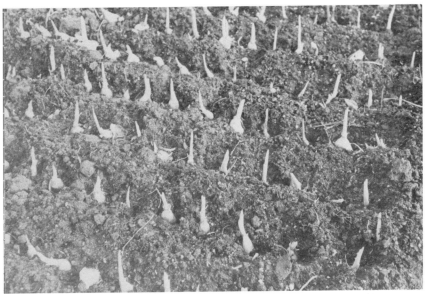

FIG 14
Corm depth at planting time is generally not critical, and shallow planting is common in the winter to make use of surface temperatures. The corms will pull themselves down to a greater depth if the soil structure is good.

There is now a good range of modern varieties which are high yielding, but an up-to-date list is impracticable since new introductions are continually being approved. The following list covers named varieties which are in general use at present:-

White	Matterhorn	Stella (Double)
	Ballerina	
	Miranda	
Cream	Morning Star	Fantasy (Double)
	Moya	
Yellow	Aurora	Himalaya (Double)
	Golden Melody	Gold Star
	Yellow River	
Red/Pink	Venus	Rosalinde (Double)
	Panama	Andes (Double)
Red/Orange	Oberon	President
	Czardas	Camera
		Alexander (Double)

Blue/Lilac	Blue Heaven	Urchida (Double)
	Cote d'Azur	Aida (Double)
	Royal Blue	Silvia (Double)

Buying Corms

Once the decision has been made as to which type of material is to be grown, it is necessary to consider buying in a suitable stock. Corms may be bought either as lifted, or after heat treatment and ready for planting. If a stock of corms is to be purchased locally it is always better to examine the growing crop before it starts to die back. In this way any virus or leaf necrosis problems can be identified, which is not possible in the case of dormant corms. Fusarium corm rot can also be spotted at this time, but this is less critical because this disease is also recognisable in dormant corms. If corms are bought in ready for planting, it is important to be sure that they have received sufficient, but not excessive, heat treatment. It is also necessary to know whether the corms have been end-treated (see below), because the time interval between receipt and the completion of planting will be more limited if this is the case.

Planting corms

On receipt from treatment, corms should be examined for soft rots and fusarium, either of which may develop in store, and then held at about 13-15°C until planted. If the corms have come directly out of heat treatment they must be planted within about four weeks. If they have had end-treatment, then that period must be deducted from the remaining time for which they can be held before planting. If the corms have been specially prepared for early flowering it is essential that they are planted without delay, and even a period of 2-3 days in transit can present problems with this technique.

Planting density will depend on the corm stock. High value named variety corms are generally planted at 6-10 per square foot (65-110 per m²) according to plant vigour and season. The wider spacings not only reduce the cost of the corms but also allow a higher corm multiplication rate so that stocks can be built up. Corms from seed are generally planted at rather higher density. As with seed, 12-14 per square foot (125-150 per m²) is suitable. Corms which have received an excessive amount of heat treatment, or which are likely to produce more than one growing point per corm for any other reason, should be planted at wider spacing than single-shoot corms. Cormlets of any size may be planted to produce a flowering crop, and it is usual to use a higher plant density for these, especially if they are being grown primarily for their corm production value. Under these conditions, a density of up to 18 per square foot (190 per m²) is acceptable for summer flowering, and a little less in the winter months.

It is usual to plant freesia corms to just cover the top of the corms with soil, but depth is not critical as the corms tend to find their own optimum depth in the early weeks of growth by using their contractile roots. However, if the surface layers of the soil are too warm for satisfactory flower bud initiation, as is likely to be the case in late spring and summer plantings, then temperature fluctuations can be reduced by planting rather deeper, say with the top of the corm at a depth of two inches. It has been shown that corms will develop quite normally if planted on their side rather than upright, even though the leaf base has to elongate further to get to the surface. This fact can be of practical value, in that it becomes possible to plant rapidly by a trenching method rather than having to place corms individually into the soil.

General culture

The culture of a corm crop is much the same as for crops grown from seed. The soil should be well watered immediately after planting, as this enables the corms to take up water lost during treatment. The soil should therefore remain quite wet for the first week after planting, before reverting to an occasional light drying back, as recommended for seedlings. This wetter period is particularly important for corms which have had end treatment or early flowering treatment, as such corms at planting time will be quite dessicated. Nutrition of corm crops should follow the same general pattern as for seed crops, applying a liquid feed when the first buds become visible, and repeating this after four to six weeks. The type of feed used depends on season, medium nitrogen being commonly employed in spring and early summer, and medium potash in autumn and winter.

The soil temperature before the start of the bud initiation stage is not critical, but should not be so low as to inhibit active root and shoot development. Conversely, high soil temperatures should be avoided, because of the difficulty of reducing these at the onset of initiation. Temperatures of the order of 12-15°C should be the target in the winter, and 15-20°C during the summer months. Cormlets, which are inclined to make rather less leaf growth than corms, should be kept a little warmer than corms, to encourage more leaf development before the onset of bud initiation. Crops with a lot of vegetative growth can be clipped over to reduce the foliage height, as described in the chapter on seed crops. The same warning applies; namely, that care must be

FIG 15
Some corm varieties have a soft foliage habit which requires more care in supporting. The variety in the foreground will be more of a problem in this respect than the one behind, which has much more upright leaves.

taken to be sure that buds have not elongated up inside the leaf sheath to the level at which cutting is to be carried out.

Bud initiation

The main cultural difference between seed and corms is in the time of flower bud initiation. In the case of corms, this phase will begin about six weeks after the end of heat treatment. This means that a corm which has received four weeks end treatment (see below) in addition to heat treatment will be ready to initiate bud within a further two weeks. Since it is essential that the corm is planted and safe from climatic fluctuations at this time if flower abnormalities are to be avoided, it is necessary to plan the treatment programme to fit in with the availability of the glasshouse and planting labour to be sure that this is possible. Under no circumstances should corms be planted more than five weeks after they have come out of heat treatment. The incidence of flower deformities would be probably such as to make a large proportion of the crop unmarketable. It is better to discard such corms, and look around for a replacement stock. The only exception should be if the corms are of high value, in which case they could still be grown on solely for their stock value rather than for cut flower production.

According to corm treatment, then, it is possible to tell quite accurately when the bud initiation stage will occur. This will generally start between two and six weeks after planting, and it can be assumed that, given the right temperature conditions, it will last for about four weeks. After buds are fully initiated temperature control need only be such as will enable growth to continue at a good rate, and can range from $10°C$ at night in winter to $20°C$ during the day in the summer months.

Temperature control during the bud initiation phase is of great importance, as has already been emphasised. The programme recommended in the previous chapter for seed crops applies equally well to corms. It must be remembered that although the bud initiation stage can last for as little as two weeks for named variety corms during low temperature conditions, it can last much longer if soil temperatures remain high. The cropping delays described for seed crops grown under summer conditions can occur similarly in corm crops, and so the various cultural techniques for reducing soil temperature in the summer described previously must be applied as necessary, and the ability to time reliably the flowering of spring and summer planted corm crops will be directly proportional to the facilities available for soil cooling. Conversely, failure to raise low soil temperatures in the winter months by heating when needed will result in the crop flowering prematurely, and yield and flower quality will also be reduced.

Corm treatment

When flowering of a corm crop is completed, then the requirements for corm ripening and lifting is exactly as described for seed-grown crops. Once the corms and cormlets are lifted they should be cleaned of dried-back roots and leaves, and sorted as required, discarding any material showing disease symptoms or physical damage. They should then be placed in wire-bottomed trays with corner spacers, and stacked for storage or treatment. The time between lifting and re-planting can vary widely according to the cropping schedule, and the only limitation is that a minimum of 13 weeks is needed for heat treatment at 30°C to break dormancy. Before heat treatment begins, the corms can be held in store. At a temperature of about 20°C this holding period can be for up to eight weeks, while a storage temperature of 1-2°C will allow up to 44 weeks before the start of heat treatment.

Holding corms at 13°C produces a rather different situation, in that corms under these conditions begin a process known as 'popping', or pupation. The old corm or cormlet transfers food material to its terminal bud, which swells to form a new corm as the old one shrivels. These 'popped' corms provide good planting material, as they have only a single growing point, and so plant density can be accurately controlled. However, there is a suggestion that popped corms may produce a lower flower quality compared with normal corms. Once the popping process has begun it must continue until a new ripened corm is fully formed, and this takes about 8-10 months. After this the popped corms are dormant, and still need the normal heat treatment before they will be able to grow actively.

Corms can also pop after heat treatment, in which case the resulting material will again become dormant, and a further heat treatment period is then needed. The heat treatment period itself, as described earlier, is basically 13 weeks at 30°C. If the corms were lifted prematurely, then they will need rather longer heat treatment, while corms left in the ground after flowering under summer conditions can be given rather shorter treatment time. In any case, up to 20 weeks may be given without any serious problems if the growing programme requires this, but damage to the terminal bud from this treatment may result in multi-headed growth in the subsequent crop.

End treatment

When corms come out of heat treatment they are in an active condition, and ready to start growing. This initial growth period will begin when the temperature drops sufficiently, whether the corms are planted or remain in store. This fact is put to advantage in the technique referred to as end treatment.

The corms, on being taken out of heat treatment at 30°C, are then left in their trays at 13°C. Humidity at this time should not be too low (75-80%). Leaf development begins, and a small shoot becomes visible, which contains the early growth stages of several leaves. Root elongation does not occur unless the humidity is very high, but root initials can be seen around the base of the corm. Up to this point, development is much the same as with corms being prepared for early flowering. In this case, however, the corms are planted before bud initiation commences, and so end treatment must not be for longer than about four weeks.

There are several situations where end treatment can be used to good advantage. One obvious one is where the glasshouse cannot be got ready in time for corms due out of heat treatment on a particular date. The period of end treatment counts towards the total time taken from coming out of heat treatment to flowering, and so the cropping schedule is not affected. End treatment is also useful where low temperature conditions would require considerable expenditure on fuel during the first month after planting. This cost can be saved with end treatment corms, although provision still has to be made for raising soil temperature to an acceptable level when planting actually takes place, otherwise premature bud initiation will occur.

The only effect of end treatment on the subsequent growth of a crop which may be of any significance is the reduction in leaf height which sometimes occurs. This happens because the early leaves initiated prior to planting tend not to elongate to the extent that they would in an actively growing plant, and so the final height they reach is less. The effect is negligible for end treatment up to three weeks, and may amount to perhaps ten percent of leaf height after four weeks treatment. This may be an advantage in conditions where bud initiation may be delayed by high temperatures, as leaf height tends to be excessive on these crops. It would, however, be an added problem in premature, low-temperature crops which would in any case have rather less than optimum leaf growth.

Early flowering treatment

Because of the expense or difficulty of achieving suitable bud initiation temperatures in certain climates, the possibility has been examined of allowing initiation to take place under controlled storage conditions before planting. This is naturally a very attractive proposition, but it is by no means a simple technique, and growers trying it for the first time should be prepared for problems. However, this method of treatment has been developed commercially both in Guernsey and in Holland, and can give reliable results. The

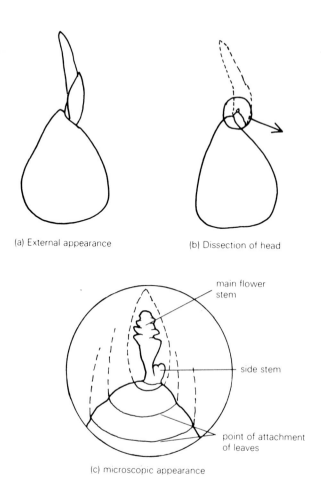

(a) External appearance   (b) Dissection of head

(c) microscopic appearance

Figure 5 Early flowering treatments – fifth week

conditions described here are tentative, and may not give such certain results as commercial early-flowering treatments.

The corms used must be in good physical condition. They should be large (say, 7cm diameter) and have a single growing point, and so they should not have received excessive heat treatment. The store climate must be controlled to a relative humidity of 90% or above, and good air movement should be maintained with fans. The high humidity encourages active vegetative growth rather than 'popping' (see later), and the air movement reduces root growth which would otherwise develop excessively in the moist conditions. The temperature regime should fluctuate between 10°C and 17°C on a twelve hour cycle, and this should be maintained for a period of six weeks, during which the

FIG 16
If foliage is to be clipped over to reduce its height, care should be taken that early buds are not already present at the cutting level. This operation is more difficult if the leaves are soft and tend to layer down onto the supports.

following observations may be made.

First week. A slight thickening of the terminal bud occurs.

Second week. The side buds on the corm start to thicken.

Third week. The terminal shoot elongates to 4-6cm.

Fourth week. Contractile roots form on the newly developing cormlets, but there is no root activity on the old corm.

At this stage, a decision must be made as to whether to continue with the treatment or to abandon it and plant out the un-initiated corms. This is because the corms must not be planted during the critical fifth or sixth weeks. This decision will be based on the physical condition of the corms after the fourth week, especially on their rate of dehydration, and this will determine whether they will come safely through the initiation phase which follows.

Fifth week. The flower bud initials are now visible microscopically, and the corms are very sensitive to climatic fluctuation at this stage.

Sixth week. Dissection should now show a visible inflorescence about 1cm long. Planting should take place immediately, as deterioration of the corms proceeds rapidly from this point onwards.

Because of the active state of the corms after this treatment they should be handled carefully during planting, avoiding damage to the developing shoots. It is important to avoid drying up of these shoots after planting, and so the crop should be regularly damped over in sunny weather, and the crop shaded from direct sun if necessary. Plenty of water should be given after planting to replace that lost during treatment, but waterlogging or panning down of the soil must be avoided.

Although accurate temperature control is not necessary after early-flowering treatment, it is still wise to avoid extremes. Low temperatures check the plant, which had just begun a good rate of active growth, while fluctuating temperatures during the first few days after planting can still give some flower deformity problems on the first cuts. Using this treatment, corms will begin to flower ten to fourteen weeks after planting. However, the side-breaks develop later in relation to the first stem, and so the total time that the crop occupies the glasshouse is not much less than a normal, well-programmed crop. The gain is in reliability of timing under less than optimum climatic conditions, rather than in the total length of the crop.

Certain modifications to this technique for early flowering may be possible, notably a combination of dry and moist storage. In this system the corms are given a normal dry end treatment of three or four weeks at 13°C, and then planted into peat in trays, using peat squares or paper pots. They are then held in a store for a further four to five weeks under suitable temperature conditions until a one centimetre bud is found on dissection, and then planted out in the glasshouse. The advantage of this method is that humidity control and air circulation requirements are avoided, as some root growth is acceptable, and so a less sophisticated store can be used, even a cellar or garage. Temperature control should still follow the programme for the more formal treatment, but some small variations should not present problems. Following this type of treatment, establishment in the bed is also easier, as the plant has a developing root system, and has not deteriorated because water uptake has already begun. This treatment can be given in the dark, as the white shoots produced green up quickly after planting. Alternatively, a low level of artificial light will keep the shoots green.

Maintenance of stocks

Freesias, whether grown from seed or from corms, have a 'bonus' income at the end of the crop in the form of a stock of corms which can be sold or re-used. The value of this bonus varies according to the stock which has been grown – seed

FIG 17
Multi-headed corm growth is often a sign of
too long heat treatment. It is important to know
if this situation is likely to occur so that corm
spacing can be planned to give a suitable
plant density.

FIG 18
Multi-headed plants give a good corm
multiplication rate, especially if the crop is left in
the ground to mature after flowering. In this case
the rate of bulking up is about eight or ten-fold.

varieties can have a rather low value, while some of the newer introductions of
named variety corms can be worth a great deal. To achieve this value, however,
it is necessary that the stock of corms should be free of disease problems – virus,
fusarium, bacterial rot, etc. This is equally important whether the stock is to be
sold off or whether it is to be retained for subsequent planting.

One of the most serious problems with freesia corms is the incidence of virus
in the stock. Its seriousness is related to the fact that it is undetectable in the
corms once they are lifted, and yet it will show itself in the early growth of the
new crop, and can spread rapidly through that crop. To maintain a stock of
corms free of virus problems it is necessary to rogue out plants in the growing
crop which display virus symptoms – whether these are leaf-streaking or flower
distortion symptoms. This roguing out must be carried right through to lifting, as
any late attack of aphid in the crop can introduce virus even at this stage.

Aphids must be controlled as soon as seen, as they will not only bring in freesia virus from other crops, but will also rapidly spread virus from an infected plant to healthy plants in the crop. If these control measures are taken methodically, then virus should not build up in a stock to any significant level. Freesia virus is not transmitted in the soil and so there is no other way in which infection can spread through a stock.

Fusarium corm rot is an equally serious disease in freesias, but for a different reason. Fusarium is carried in the soil, and in old corms which have rotted in the crop and so have not been lifted, and is extremely difficult to eradicate. The symptoms of fusarium infection in a freesia plant are easily identified, and immediate and regular roguing is essential. The best way to use fungicides to control fusarium in a growing crop and the alternative methods of soil sterilisation between crops are described in later chapters. Soft rot of corms is a problem which can remain quite insignificant in a production area for several years, and then suddenly increase to the stage when stocks are being quite seriously infected. The conditions under which corms are handled prior to going into treatment can have a significant effect on the subsequent spread of soft rot in a stock, and once the disease is present in a proportion of corms in a batch, then it can spread rapidly through that batch under the conditions which obtain during heat treatment.

It is recommended that, to reduce the risk of rot in a stock of corms, the corms should be lifted when the foliage is still green, but preferably not until two or three weeks after flowering has finished, so that the corm has time to mature. The leaves should then be removed immediately, rather than the whole plants being hung up or stacked for a period after lifting. This is particularly important at this time of the year when high temperatures in the glasshouse can cause the plants to lose water rapidly, which softens the corms and makes them more susceptible to the spread of bacterial rot. This technique is a compromise, to the extent that new cormlet development takes place largely after flowering, and so a smaller number of useable cormlets will be obtained by lifting the stock early in this way. In the case of a low value seed stock this will probably be acceptable, but where a good multiplication rate is important, as in the case of expensive named variety corms, the crop may be left in the ground rather longer if soft rot is not a problem. During the cleaning of the stock any corms showing damage or softness should be discarded.

If the problems described above are kept in mind when handling stocks of corms, then these stocks will realise their proper value as a part of the economics of freesia growing. If stocks are lost as the result of avoidable diseases being allowed to develop in the corms then not only is their value lost, but also a new problem follows — the need to buy in new stocks, with the consequent risk of introducing further disease at the same time. This is a vicious circle which the freesia grower should take all necessary steps to avoid.

5: Aspects of Crop Management

Little has been said in previous chapters about general cultural requirements in the way of watering, spraying over, ventilation, etc., apart from the importance of these techniques for soil cooling during the bud initiation period. Although freesias are basically an easy crop to grow, it is still important to understand the fundamentals of plant growth to be sure that growing conditions allow the full potential of the crop to be achieved.

Water balance

One of the most important plant processes as far as growing conditions are concerned is that known as transpiration. Transpiration is the controlled loss of water from the leaves, and is largely responsible in turn for the uptake of water and nutrients by the plant. The roots actively take up water, and so transpiration and root activity have to be properly balanced if correct water relationships within the plant are to be maintained. If this water balance is not maintained, a number of cultural problems of commercial importance can follow. If water uptake and loss get out of step, flower stems may dry back, or crack and break in a horizontal plane, and in severe cases the foliage may also wilt. Fluctuations in water balance are also the cause of bent flower stems, since a reduction in water content makes them soften and droop, and subsequent development of the tissues makes the bend irreversible, even when water balance later improves.

To maintain a healthy, actively growing crop it is necessary to encourage both root action and transpiration, and at the same time to prevent one from continuing in the absence of the other. The symptoms of poor root action in relation to transpiration are described above. Root action which is excessive in conditions where transpiration is low can similarly give problems. This commonly happens in corm crops which are planted in cold, humid conditions. Root activity continues, but is not matched by water loss from the leaves, and the developing leaves then become stunted and deformed. The leaves never recover completely, and produce the condition known as 'curlers'.

To encourage good water balance in the plants it is necessary to provide suitable conditions —a strong, clean root system, moist but not water-logged soil, warmth, and a low enough humidity in the air for the plants to be able to release water vapour from the leaves. The first essential, a good root system, is easily achieved if the soil structure is good and the soil is free of root rot diseases. The secret is to allow the soil near the surface to dry back a little between waterings during the early stages of growth. This encourages the plant to make a larger root system to search for water. This drying back does not need to be at all extreme.

Soil temperature is equally important in maintaining active growth. Applying heat as necessary during the winter months to keep a mean soil temperature around 10-13°C keeps the crop ticking over, and will probably have only a low fuel requirement. Temperatures a little lower, say 8-10°C, may be necessary in areas of poor winter light, to avoid pale, drawn plants and weak bud development. Perhaps the factors which are of greatest significance in encouraging the plants to remain active are those which encourage transpiration – these include ventilation, pipe heat, and damping down. The object is to maintain a humidity which is low enough to allow water-loss from the leaves to the atmosphere, but not so low as to cause water to be lost faster than it can be replaced by root action.

Table 1 summarises the action which should be taken to maintain suitable humidity under various climatic conditions.

WEATHER	NATURAL HUMIDITY LEVEL	VENTILATE	DAY PIPE HEAT	SPRAY OVER CROP
Dull, damp and calm	Very high	A little at all times	Yes – very important	No
Dull, but windy	High/medium	A little at all times	Yes	No
Bright, but calm	Medium/low	Start to open early	Not necessary	Yes – occasionally
Bright and windy	Very low	Start to open before sunrise	Not necessary	Frequently (and water more often)

TABLE 1. REQUIREMENTS FOR HUMIDITY CONTROL

The object is simple – to provide conditions in which water uptake by the roots remains active, and is balanced by transpiration loss from the leaves. In this way the plants remain in a good state of active water balance, and is better able to withstand any unavoidable climatic changes which may occur.

FIG 19
'Curlers' developing in a corm crop where air temperatures are too low, especially in high humidity conditions. Some varieties are particularly susceptible to this problem.

Flower deformities

The factors which produce flower deformities have already been discussed, but it is worthwhile here listing the various forms of abnormality which can occur, together with their causes. Firstly, there are the three related deformities in the inflorescence brought about by excessive temperature fluctuations, or other variations in the environment, during the bud initiation stage.

Thumbing is the condition where the first bud on the stem is separated from the others by a longer than normal length of stem. In extreme cases this bud may be as much as ten centimetres below the head, and the second and third buds may be similarly affected. When severe thumbing occurs it is often possible to remove the displaced bud before marketing.

Gladiolus bloom is the name given for the failure of the flower head to turn through a right angle, so resulting in a vertical flower head similar to that found in gladioli.

Bracting describes the condition of the flower head where the bracts, which are the small green leaves at the base of each bud, elongate excessively, and give a wheat-ear appearance to the head.

These three types of deformity may occur in any combination in varying degrees of severity, and can result either in down-grading or in unmarketability of the blooms. Because of the origin of the problem in the bud initiation stage, there is no corrective action which can be taken when it is seen. It is often the case that the earliest blooms cut from a crop show some flower abnormalities, but that these practically disappear as the crop bulks up.

FIG 20
The loss of leaf area which results from the physiological disorder known as 'curlers' can be clearly seen here. This leaf area is never fully recovered, and a stunted crop with consequently a low yield is the outcome.

Blind buds, where the tail of the inflorescence fails to develop, sometimes occur, and these are caused by either low light intensity or by dessication after excessively high temperatures following bud initiation. Other flower abnormalities include virus distortion or flecking, damage caused by various insect pests (see chapter eight) and stem cracking or bending brought about by fluctuating water balance within the plants.

Soil sterilisation

The frequency and method of soil sterilisation for freesias will depend on the problems with which the sterilisation has to cope. For crops grown in clean soil, particularly corm crops, sterilisation after every second crop is often sufficient. Where fusarium has been identified in a crop, then sterilisation should be carried out between each crop. There are two basic alternatives for sterilising the soil. Firstly, steam sterilisation, which can be carried out in a number of different ways (grids, pans or sheet steaming, for example) with different degrees of effectiveness depending on the depth of penetration and the time for which the steam temperature is maintained. If old corms remain in the soil a long time is needed to be sure that any disease harboured in these corms is reached and eliminated. When the temperature throughout the soil has reached 100°C, the 'cook' should be maintained for a further 30-45 minutes.

Secondly, chemical soil sterilants can be used. In particular, methyl bromide gas application is often employed for freesias, as it gives good control of weeds, insects and root rot fungi, and some degree of control over fusarium, although steaming is generally preferred for fusarium control. Other chemical sterilants are sometimes used, and these are listed in table 2.

STERILANT	PEST OR DISEASE				
	Weeds	Root Knot Eelworm	Root Rots	Fusarium	Insects
Steam	Good	Good	Good	Good	Good
Cresylic Acid	No	Fair	No	No	Good
Formaldehyde	Fair	No	Fair	Fair	No
Metham Sodium	Good	Fair	Good	Good	Good
Methyl Iso-thio-cyanide (MIC)	Good	Fair	Good	Good	Good
Dazomet	Good	Fair	Good	Good	Good
Chloropicrin	No	No	Good	Good	Fair
Ethylene Di-bromide	No	Good	No	No	Fair
D – D	No	Good	No	No	No
Nabam	No	No	Good	Fair	No
Methyl Bromide	Fair	Good	Fair	Fair	Good
MIC + DD	Good	Good	Good	Good	Good
E.D.B. + Chloropicrin	No	Good	Good	Good	Fair

TABLE 2. SPECTRUM OF ACTIVITY OF SOIL STERILANTS

The release of these chemicals must be carefully carried out, as any residue can cause crop damage. Wet soils, and soils high in organic matter will retain chemicals for longer than other soils. The time intervals quoted by manu-

FIG 21
This sequence illustrates the range of 'thumbing' and 'gladiolus bloom' which can be caused by faulty temperature control during the bud initiation stage.

facturers should be strictly adhered to, and a longer time allowed if conditions require this.

Weed control

Although weed control should generally be thought of as part of the soil sterilisation programme, there are particular situations where the use of chemical weedkillers must be considered. For cleaning up around the glasshouse and on standing-out ground, weeds may be burned off with paraquat. However, freesias are particularly sensitive to contact damage with this chemical, and great care should be taken to avoid spray drift on to a growing crop. Where certain perennial weeds are a problem the weedkiller glyphosate can be used to advantage where time permits, as it is translocated down to the roots to give long-term control. Like paraquat, it should only be used in non-crop situations.

Generally speaking, no weedkiller should be used on a growing crop of freesias, as trials have shown that even where no visible damage is observed there may be a significant yield reduction. However, where annual weed

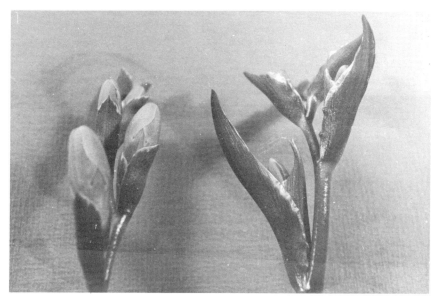

FIG 22
'Bracting', caused by elongation of the green bracts below each flower bud, can cause downgrading or rejection of blooms. Again, this is caused by excessively fluctuating temperatures while the bud is being initiated.

seedlings are expected to cause serious problems in corm crops the material chloroxuron may be considered. It should be applied to weed-free soils about 4-6 weeks after planting, and will then control germinating seedlings for two or three months if used carefully according to the manufacturer's recommendations. In particular, chloroxuron should be applied in overcast conditions and the crop should be lightly sprayed over with water after application. In the case of seed crops, there is no satisfactory alternative to good soil sterilisation before sowing. Clean soil is necessary in any case to avoid the risk of root rots and similar problems on the young seedlings.

Soilless growing media

Freesias can be grown in soilless media, thus doing away with the uncertainties of soil sterilisation. However, there are particular problems which then have to be considered, notably in relation to nutrient and salt levels and fluoride toxicity. Peat culture has been attempted in Guernsey on several occasions, but the degree of success often leaves something to be desired. The greatest problem here is probably one of leaf scorch caused by fluoride uptake (see below), but

FIG 23
Bent flower stems are generally caused by variable water balance within the plant. Temporary wilting which develops if the roots cannot replace water lost by the leaves sets into a permanent curve as the cells in the flower stem mature.

fluctuating nutrient and salt levels have also to be considered. Because raw peat has no appreciable nutrient content, base fertilisers and lime have to be added before use. A suitable formula is given in appendix 2. This provides suitable starting levels, but when the crop is growing and being regularly watered – at least daily watering with liquid feed is necessary during the summer months – nutrient balance can change rapidly because of the varying degrees of solubility and mobility of nutrients in peat substrates. In particular, potash and nitrate levels can fall rapidly, while sodium, which is not necessary to the crop and causes problems by adding to the overall salt content of the medium, builds up if it occurs in the water supply because it is much less easily leached.

Because of these difficulties, it is suggested that growing freesias in soilless substrates, especially peat, should not be considered on a commercial scale until small-scale trials have been carried out to examine the problems. In particular, two requirements need to be met before peat culture is used – a clean water supply, with low sodium and fluoride levels, and an analytical service to enable frequent checks on the nutrient status of the substrate to be made.

Crop housing

Crops which are grown outside in pots during the early stages and which are to be brought in to the glasshouse for flowering should be moved inside in time for the plants to root in to the border soil. Generally the root growth in containers is

FIG 24
Light and dark banding on the flower stem is a sign of over-vigorous growth, and is often accompanied by thick stems, as seen here. This fault is encouraged by feeding with high nitrogen fertilisers.

not enough to support good development of the later side-breaks, so yield and quality are reduced if housing is delayed. The correct time to house freesias is when the first bud is seen. Pots should be placed on to moist soil, preferably with a little peat incorporated into the top inch or two, and watering through the pot should be gradually reduced as root emerges into the bed. Particular care should be taken to avoid high salt levels in the border soil, as this will discourage rooting out and result in a weak, stunted crop.

Frost damage

Although freesias can be grown through the winter months with only a minimum temperature requirement, they are still sensitive to frost damage, and air temperatures should not be allowed to drop below freezing. An air minimum of −3°C is low enough to cause severe crop damage, particularly when this is followed by a sunny day with low humidity.

The symptom most commonly observed is found in crops showing bud. The stem of the bud softens and droops, and then falls over at a point a little way below the head. The exact point of collapse depends on the stage of maturity of the stem, and if the first floret is already showing colour then the collapse may be limited to the tip of the flower head. More severe frosting will also affect the leaves, particularly the younger leaves. These turn grey and almost translucent as the cells collapse, and eventually turn blue and die back. Neither stems nor

FIG 25
The first, and most commonly observed, symptom of frost damage in freesias is the toppling of the flower stem a short way behind the head. This occurs as water withdrawal from the actively growing cells in this region causes their collapse.

leaves affected in this way will recover as the plant cell walls become ruptured at the time of damage.

The obvious way to avoid frost damage to freesias is of course to apply heat to prevent temperatures falling to the danger level, but where this cannot be done, either because the structure has no heating system or because of a breakdown, then there are certain measures which can be taken to reduce the damage. Firstly, it is possible to reduce the extent to which the frost gets into the crop and to maintain humidity. This can be done by lining the sides of the house with clear polythene, or by covering over the crop with polythene, hessian, or even newspaper. Secondly, and probably more important, steps can be taken to reduce the sudden changes in humidity, and therefore water balance within the plants, which follow frost conditions.

This can be done by applying water over the top of the crop first thing in the morning, so maintaining a good moisture level in the atmosphere. This is particularly important when clear skies and consequent low humidities are expected. If it is intended to apply ventilation on a sunny morning it is essential to spray over before opening up, and to open before the sun hits the glasshouse if at all possible.

FIG 26
Frosting of the foliage can occur in serious cases, and this shows initially as a transparency of the leaves, as illustrated here. Eventually these leaves dry back and become straw-coloured.

Fluoride toxicity

Freesias are particularly sensitive to leaf scorch caused by the uptake of fluoride. The symptom is a scorch on the tips and edges of the leaves, particularly visible on the older leaves. The irregular scorched patches are often orange-brown in colour, giving rise to the Dutch name 'fire' for the disorder. Fluoride uptake may be from the atmosphere by the leaves — industrial pollution will produce this effect — or from the soil or growing medium by root uptake. Fluoride contamination of the soil may come about in several ways. Many phosphate fertilisers, including superphosphate, have fluoride as an impurity, and so contribute to fluoride levels in the soil when used as base fertilisers. The water used for irrigation purposes may also have a significant level of fluoride. The 1 p.p.m. level applied to domestic water supplies in some parts of the UK, for example, is enough to cause scorch symptoms, while natural levels in some regions may be even higher than this. Fluoride-containing glass cleaning agents will also contribute to the overall level of fluoride in the soil, and should be avoided.

The symptom of fluoride toxicity is more likely to appear in soils or other substrates where either the pH or the calcium level is low. Because of this, soils should be limed wherever these levels are border-line, and top-dressings of carbonate of lime may be used to reduce the development of fluoride toxicity symptoms. The common occurrence of leaf scorch symptoms in crops grown in peat is likely to be induced by conditions encouraging fluoride uptake. Peat substrates are generally quite acid, and have rather low calcium levels. Also, superphosphate is often used as a phosphate source. To compensate for this,

FIG 27
Fluoride toxicity exhibits itself as a marginal scorch of the older leaves. This is often an orange-brown colour.

the formula for the peat substrate given in appendix 2 recommends quite a high level of carbonate of lime in comparison with that used for most other crops. Because of the risk of fluoride contamination causing leaf scorch, it is recommended that peat used for soil conditioning before planting or sowing freesias should be used only in moderation, and should be accompanied by an adequate level of lime to keep the pH up to 6.5 or higher.

Tissue culture

Although the multiplication of freesias in the laboratory by tissue culture is not at the present time of any great commercial value, a brief description may be of interest. The technique is designed to produce a large number of plants from a single plant, thus developing a 'clone' in much the same way as normal corm multiplication does to produce named varieties. In the case of freesias this is achieved by taking the immature flower stem of the plant and culturing it in a particular environment on an agar-based medium. This encourages the development of masses of undifferentiated cell tissue known as callus. The callus can then be either sub-cultured or transferred to a new medium, following which it begins to produce plantlets. These plantlets are then transferred to glasshouse conditions and grown on in the normal way.

Although the method has been developed to the point of being reliable under laboratory conditions, it is not without its problems, and its future value as a commercial technique remains in doubt at the present time. Its potential use in short-cutting the multiplication plase of new variety production may be offset by the fact that several years' selection and trialling of new material is in any case needed to evaluate its potential under a range of cultural conditions.

6: Picking, Bunching and Marketing

The various techniques used for preparing freesia blooms for marketing depend largely on particular market requirements, and so it is not possible to lay down inflexible rules to cover all situations. In general, the information covered in this chapter will refer to crops grown for the United Kingdom markets, and growers elsewhere will have to modify this according to their own needs.

Picking

Freesias are most commonly picked by cutting through the stem with a knife. The position of the cut will depend on the market. For the UK, where extra stem length does not produce a good premium, it is usual to cut down only to just above the next marketable side-break. This may involve cutting past one or more unmarketable breaks, and these are stripped off before bunching. For this system of cutting, a marketable stem may be considered as one having a length of twenty centimetres or more, and a minimum of five normally-developing florets, although these criteria will depend on the overall quality of the crop, the variety, and the strength of the market. This is the usual cutting method in Guernsey, and is the basis of the information given in chapter seven on crop yields.

In Holland there is much greater emphasis on stem length, and the premium obtained for blooms with a good stem (over 40cm) warrants a different harvesting system. Here, the stem is cut down to the required length, even if this involves cutting past good side-breaks, and these breaks are left on the stem as a bonus to the buyer. As a result of this cutting method, Dutch freesia growers place a considerable emphasis on the height of side-breaks on the main stem when evaluating new varieties. They also require a narrow angle between the side-break and the main stem as this produces a more attractive product when cut in this way. Although this cutting technique does give a better quality product, and the stem length complements the better quality blooms of the named variety stocks grown in the Netherlands, it does of course reduce marketable yield to some extent, and whether or not it is economic to cut in this way will depend on whether the market premium achieved compensates for the yield loss.

The stage of picking varies with the time which will be taken for the stems to get to market and then to the consumer, and also with climatic conditions, since the rate of bud opening depends on the temperature. For local direct sales, particularly in the winter, the stems will probably be cut with the first floret fully open and the second cracking. At the other extreme, blooms cut in the summer, and which will take, say, four days to reach the consumer (as may happen with Guernsey freesias sold through UK markets) will need to be cut at a very immature stage.

Bud opening

There is a limit to the degree of immaturity at which a freesia may be safely cut, as the later florets on the stem may fail to open under some conditions. As a general rule, the first floret should be about to crack open at the tip to avoid such problems and to guarantee a reasonable vase life. The greatest risk with buds opening poorly after cutting occurs in the poor light conditions of winter, and so this problem is not one which is commonly found in practice, since crops are generally cut less tight at this time than during the summer.

Proprietary materials are available which can be used to increase the proportion of buds which will subsequently open on stems which are cut at an immature stage. Although the vase life of freesias does depend considerably on the stage at which the buds are cut, growers may have to cut immature stems at particular times; for example, on Fridays to cover the weekend period if no labour is available at that time. A commercial bud opening solution is of value in such a situation. The stems are immersed in the solution shortly after cutting, and left at a temperature between 10-20°C until they reach the normal cutting stage. If they need to be stored beyond this time, then a cold store is advisable. This can run at 2°C, at which temperature the further development of the buds is greatly slowed down, but not completely stopped.

The frequency of picking will depend on the time of year and the marketing arrangements. In the winter, cutting over weekly may be sufficient for some crops, while during the high temperatures of summer it may be barely adequate to cut over daily. Particularly in the summer, blooms should be cut in the morning, before the plant can become soft, and stored in a cool place in water until bunching. In this way, the crop can be damped down after picking to keep up the humidity and so maintain active growth. Depending on marketing methods, a cold store to hold the flowers after cutting may be a worthwhile investment, although a cool cellar or similar may do almost as well in some

FIG 28
Stems should not be cut at an earlier stage than the one illustrated here. A less mature stem may fail to open the later buds. In the winter, a more fully opened first bloom may be required, according to marketing arrangements.

FIG 29
The standard bunching system in Guernsey involves selecting five stems to form the basic unit. These need not be the same length, but the bases should be made level.

FIG 30
The bunch of five stems are then put into a tapered polythene sleeve. This machine, using a fan to open out the sleeves for simple access, is commonly used.

FIG 31
The base of each stem should protrude beyond the end of the sleeve so that it can later be wrapped in a moistened water-absorbent pad (or 'sock') to provide for water uptake in transit.

FIG 32
Five sleeved bunches are then put together to make up the unit which is boxed. These five bunches are then held together with the 'sock', which is held on by a small rubber band.

FIG 33
A number of these 5 x 5 bunches are then boxed up for shipment, held in place by a wooden or metal
'pin-stick'. Eight or ten units of this size are most usually put in, giving a box count of 200-250 blooms.

situations. The holding temperature is not critical, and cool stores are usually run at about 2-10°C, depending on how long the flowers need to be held before shipment.

Bunching

Freesias are most commonly sold bunched in either fives or tens. Whether they are bunched in separate colours or mixed will depend on the material being grown and on market needs. Of course, named variety stocks will be marketed separately in most cases, since their principal advantage lies in their uniformity, although there are a few growers who grow named varieties in a range of colours for mixed bunching. Seed strains, and corms produced from seed strains, may be grown in separate colours or mixed. In either case, it is usual to make up a mixed bunch for marketing, since the uniformity of shade and flower shape within a colour is not sufficient to justify marketing individual colours, with the possible exception of whites.

The actual balance of colour within the bunch may have to be modified to fit in with production at any particular time, but as a general rule a well-constructed bunch may consist of two yellows, one white (or a third yellow), and one each of blue and red/pink. The dominance of the lighter colours is generally most acceptable to the consumer. Because of this, mixed colour seed strains are usually made up in the proportion 30-40% yellow, 10% white and up to 20% each red, pink and blue, to allow for such a colour balance in the product. Where separate colour stocks are being used for mixed bunching, then the proportions of each colour should follow this pattern.

The bunch of five or ten stems may be held together in one of several ways. The simplest is to place a small rubber band over the stems. If the cut ends are to be wrapped in a water-holding material, then the band should be placed high up the stems. Conversely, if the stems are to be held together with tapered sleeves, then the band should be around the base of the stems. Alternatively, the stems may be bound together with tape or nylon thread either by hand or by the use of a bunch tying machine which performs this operation. If tapered sleeves and wrapping of the cut ends are both used, then it is possible to dispense with the rubber band or thread completely.

Grading

The market will determine whether quality grading is necessary, and also how it should be carried out. A particular standard may be set for first grade blooms, and any material of a lower standard may be marketed separately or discarded. A suitable first-grade standard for seed-strain freesias, which is generally accepted by UK Markets, is described as follows:

'Produce must be of good quality, and all parts of the cut flowers must be whole, fresh, and free from pest and disease symptoms, chemical residues, bruising and growth defects. Stems must be rigid, and strong enough to support the flower head. They should be reasonably straight, and should have a minimum length of 20 centimetres. The flower head should contain at least five buds capable of opening in water. A tolerance of five per cent may be acceptable.'

In addition to this first grade, there may also be an Extra Quality grade, based on longer stems (say, over 30cm) and more buds (say, at least seven). The phrase 'growth defects' in the above standard is particularly important, since a proportion of flower deformities is found in all crops. These defects, known as 'gladiolus bloom', 'thumbing' and 'bracting', are described in chapter five, and suitable cultural conditions should be applied to the crop to avoid a high percentage of these flower abnormalities.

Quality requirements for mainland Europe, as has already been noted, are rather more demanding; with a particular emphasis on stem length. A first grade stem for this market should be 45cm or more, and a second grade bloom 35-45cm long. This requires the Dutch cutting method described above, and may reduce total yield considerably, depending on crop vigour and variety. Grading standards may be different for particular varieties. For example, a double-flowering variety such as Fantasy has fewer flower buds on each stem, and four or five buds may represent first grade stems in this case.

Transport

The need for a packing system will clearly depend on whether the freesias are to be sold locally or have to be transported some distance to market. In Holland, blooms sent through the auctions are generally transported by road to their final destination, and reach the retail outlet in most cases within 24-36 hours after being picked. Moreover, they are transported in custom-built air conditioned vehicles, and so protection to the blooms can be minimal. Because of this, freesias marketed in this way can be packed dry in loose boxes, bunched in tens, and tied with twine.

In the case of Guernsey, transport conditions are very different. Cut freesias have to be carried by air to various points in the United Kingdom, taken by road to the wholesale markets, and then again by road to the retail outlets. The journey from nursery to point-of-sale for Guernsey freesias may take three or more days, and involve the blooms being loaded or unloaded on eight occasions. Because of this it is necessary to pack the blooms securely into containers, and to provide them with water in transit. This latter requirement is met by packing a moistened water-holding material such as cotton wool around the cut ends of the stem before packing. This is held in place with a rubber band. Proprietary 'socks' can be obtained, ready cut to size, which consist of an inner layer of absorbent material and an outer layer of polythene to prevent loss of water by evaporation.

Currently, the most common bunching system in Guernsey involves banding the freesias in fives, and then combining five bunches of five stems in a single 'sock'. Eight or ten of these multiple units are then packed into a cardboard box, lined with water-resistant paper,and fastened into place with various types of pin sticks which prevent the bunches from moving in transit. This gives a count of 200-250 stems in a box measuring 450x300x130mm. The majority of freesias leaving Guernsey are protected by transparent polyethylene tapered sleeves, which take a single bunch of five stems. These sleeves provide a more attractive product than an unsleeved bunch, and their cost may be justified by additional market value. Tapered sleeves can be put onto bunches by hand, or a fan-operated sleeving machine is available commerically which reduces the labour requirement of this aspect of packing.

Picking, bunching and packing represents a large part of the total labour requirement for growing freesias, and so the total labour input for the crop will range widely according to whether the crop is sold locally through direct outlets, or whether it has to be transported some distance.

7: Crop Programmes and Costings

Having considered how to grow freesias, we must now decide on a crop programme to give the required pattern of production, and look at some economic aspects of commercial freesia production. We will first look at crop timings, since it is essential to know when and over what period crops started at different times of the year will flower. Then we will consider crop yields in relation to season, since there is considerable natural variation in potential production levels from month to month, and this is likely to influence the choice of crop programme. Finally we will look at production costs, fuel requirements, and labour input, so that these may be set against possible returns to assess profitability.

Crop timing

The time taken from sowing seed or planting corms to the start of picking, and the length of the picking period itself, vary widely according to the season. This is brought about by a combination of factors, the most important of which is the temperature regime for flower bud initiation. By making a number of assumptions it is possible to draw up a table which will indicate crop timing according to the time of planting or sowing. The basis of this information is a series of trials which were carried out by the Guernsey Horticultural Advisory Service several years ago, in which seed was sown, and corms planted (with and without end-treatment) at monthly intervals throughout an eighteen month period. The conclusions from these trials have since been supported by observations made on many commercial crops.

To consider seed-grown crops first, we must assume that germination is rapid and uniform, and that no subsequent check to normal growth occurs other than that produced by climatic conditions. The temperatures in the trial were held to a minimum of 10-13°C during the winter months by means of a hot water system, and, conversely, all normal cultural methods for keeping soil temperatures down (ventilation, shading and damping down) were applied throughout the summer. The glasshouse used was not custom-built, and so crop timing in modern structures with soil warming, soil cooling and extra ventilation may be rather different.

The time taken from sowing to the first commercial pick under conditions described can be estimated from the following table.

SOWN	WEEKS TO PICK	SOWN	WEEKS TO PICK
January	18-21	July	25-32
February	19-22	August	23-28
March	21-24	September	22-26
April	23-27	October	21-24
May	25-32	November	20-22
June	27-35	December	19-21

TABLE 3. TIME FROM SOWING SEED TO START OF PICKING

The range quoted allows for the natural variation in climate found in Guernsey, but makes no provision for much greater extremes which may well occur elsewhere. In particular, cool sea breezes keep summer temperatures down to a lower level in Guernsey than would be found on the European mainland, and so crops initiating bud during the summer may be subject to greater delays where temperatures are higher. Even in Guernsey conditions, crops due to flower in September-October can be delayed until the following January or February if the summer and early autumn remain continuously hot.

Particular cultural conditions will require modifications to the information in the table. For example, in the case of seed pre-germinated at high temperature during the winter months, there is a reduction in total growing time because germination and emergence may be as much as three weeks quicker than direct sown seed with a lower temperature regime. By calculating the period during which crops grown from seed are sensitive to bud initiation factors (see chapter three) it is possible to predict any variation in crop timing which would result if mean soil temperatures during this stage were significantly lower or higher than normal for the time of year. In the same way, application of a particular temperature regime at the bud initiation stage may be used to deliberately change crop timing. However, it must be remembered that temperatures outside the recommended range may have the side effect of giving lower yield or poorer quality.

For crops grown from corms, the same principles apply, but the period from planting to first commercial pick will be considerably less than that for seed crops.

PLANTED	WEEKS TO PICK		PLANTED	WEEKS TO PICK
January	14-17		July	18-24
February	14-17		August	19-25
March	14-17		September	18-23
April	14-17		October	17-21
May	14-17		November	16-20
June	15-19		December	15-18

TABLE 4. TIME FROM PLANTING CORMS TO START OF PICKING

Here, the term 'planting' is not really correct, because these timings refer only to corms planted directly out of heat treatment. In the case of end-treated corms, the length of end treatment can be deducted from the total growing period indicated in the table, to obtain the real time from planting to picking. For example, corms planted in June and which had received four weeks end treatment would have come out of heat treatment in May, and will crop in 14-17 weeks from that time (10-13 weeks after planting). The table in any case gives only an approximation, which will vary both with climate and with variety.

Harvesting period

The length of the flowering period depends on total yield and on temperature. Since the yield can vary by a factor of three or more according to the time of year and the variety, then the harvesting period can also range widely. For crops grown from seed of from corm-from-seed, the lack of uniformity results in a longer flowering period than for named variety corms. Named variety corms with a yield as low as 1-1½ stems per plant can flower over as short a time as three or four weeks, while a seed crop with a similar yield will need between nine and twelve weeks according to temperature. Corms from seed generally have a shorter harvesting period than crops grown from the same strain of seed, because there is a shorter growing period before bud initiation, and so less opportunity for variations in timing to be magnified during this stage.

FLOWERING TIME	YIELD	SEED	CORMS-FROM-SEED	NAMED VARIETIES
	1-2 stems/plant	9-11	7-9	3-6
Summer	2-3 stems/plant	11-14	9-12	5-9
	3-4 stems/plant	13-17	11-15	7-12
	1-2 stems/plant	10-12	8-10	4-7
Winter	2-3 stems/plant	12-16	10-14	6-10
	3-4 stems/plant	14-20	12-18	8-14

TABLE 5. WEEKS OF COMMERCIAL PICKING

FIG 34
Flower quality can vary considerably according to the temperature regime at bud initiation, and also according to the time of year. Both the number and the quality of the buds on the stem, as well as stem length and strength, can vary.

Crop programming

To build up a programme of crop timings, three phases have to be added together. Firstly, the period from sowing or planting has to be estimated from the appropriate tables, making due allowances for pre-germination of seed or end-treatment of corms, and for any significant climatic differences from the conditions under which the information in the tables was obtained. In particular, care has to be exercised when predicting the flowering time of any crop which is expected to initiate bud shortly before the onset of summer conditions. Secondly, the harvesting period as predicted above must be added on, using an appropriate yield estimate (see below). Finally, time must be allowed for corm ripening after the conclusion of flowering. This can be as much as eight weeks where the production of cormlets is important, or as little as two weeks if the corms are to be dried off out of the ground.

The total period obtained from these calculations gives an indication of how long the glasshouse will be occupied by a particular crop, but allowance must also be made for the time taken to lift and clear the corms, for soil sterilisation, and for house preparation for the following crop. To give two examples relevant to Guernsey conditions, seed sown in April should need about 25 weeks to come into flower, and, on a yield estimate of three stems per plant, a further 15 weeks of cropping. Then, allowing eight weeks for corm ripening and four weeks glasshouse turn-round, the total time needed for this crop is a full year. On the other hand, named variety corms planted in October with a likely yield of 1½ stems per plant will probably flower in 18-19 weeks, and crop for about five weeks, so that the total glasshouse utilisation period in this case will only be about seven or eight months.

Predicted yields

Although it is possible to plan programmes of freesia production to flower at any time of the year on the basis of the information given above, the profitability of any programme will still depend to a large extent on yield. This is because there is a large variation in potential yield according to the time of year. Therefore the yield factor has to be taken into account at the planning stage. Because of this seasonal yield variation, true year-round production may not be a profitable exercise in freesia growing, and neither may it be good economy to have the greenhouse occupied to its maximum through the year, because in each case to do so may require growing a crop through the time of the year when potential production is low. However, the need to maintain a uniform labour input may in some situations compensate for occasional less-than-optimum yields.

As with the information given on crop-timing, the potential yield figures given below are based on trials in Guernsey. Because it is not clear what causes the considerable variation from month to month it is not possible to predict how the pattern may differ in other growing areas. Work is in progress at the present time in an attempt to identify the factors which cause this effect. It appears to be related in some way to changes in day length, and so it is unlikely that the pattern can be significantly altered by cultural techniques, as would be possible if it were a temperature factor, for example.

SOWN OR PLANTED	SEED	CORMS-FROM-SEED
January	3	3
February	4	3½
March	4	4
April	3	4
May	2	4
June	2	2½
July	1½	2
August	1½	2
September	1½	1½
October	2	1½
November	2	2
December	3	2½

TABLE 6 POTENTIAL YIELD IN STEMS PER PLANT

The figures are based on the tetraploid seed strains commercially available a few years ago, and so recently introduced strains may be slightly different in their yield capabilities. Named variety corms vary widely in yield. Low yielding varieties such as the double-flowered Fantasy seldom produces above 1½-2 stems per plant, while some newer introductions may yield as heavily as good seed strains. Cormlets in most cases would be expected to yield a little less than corms of the same strain or variety. In all the figures given, a plant density of 10-12 per square foot is assumed, and much wider spacings, as may be used with high-value corms, may yield proportionally more stems per plant. Thus, some recent named varieties are quoted as yielding ten or more stems per plant with a plant spacing of about 13 centimetres square (50-60 plants per square metre), and under optimum growing conditions.

Costs of production

Because of the variation in production costs between growing areas, and also the rate at which costs change from year to year, it is not practicable to give actual figures. However, the list of materials and other costs involved in freesia growing is not great, and the grower can quickly calculate his own costs of production for any particular crop programme according to local costs. To help in this exercise, the following notes offer a breakdown of the main headings of costs in freesia production, although the extent to which any one item is applicable to a particular growing programme will depend on several factors.

Direct costs	**Marketing costs**	**Capital costs**
Seed or corms	Boxes	Glasshouse utilisation
Corm treatment	Lining paper	Irrigation and other equipment
Pots/compost for pre-	Bands, twine, tape	Crop supports
germinating seed	Tapered sleeves	Corm trays
Fertilisers and liquid feed	Pin-sticks	Seedling boxes
Soil conditioning materials	Freight	Corm treatment facilities
Pesticides and weedkillers	Sales commission	Bunching or packing
Soil sterilisation		equipment
Fuel		Shading materials (e.g.
Water		hessian)
Electricity		
Labour		
Sundries		

Two of these items in particular may require amplification, fuel costs and labour requirements, since each constitutes a major part of the total production costs, and each may vary widely with the cropping programme.

Fuel consumption

Fuel may be needed for three purposes in freesia growing. Firstly, to provide suitable soil temperatures for the bud initiation stage when this occurs during the winter months. Secondly, to give suitable growing conditions for any stage of the crop such as to maintain active growth in low temperature periods, and to encourage air movement through the crop to prevent the spread of botrytis and other diseases in damp conditions. Thirdly, to produce steam for soil sterilisation. The first two requirements for fuel allow consumption to be calculated provided the mean outside air temperatures and the target glasshouse temperature regime are both known.

For example, to achieve a constant temperature regime of 13°C when the mean outside air temperature is 8°C requires a fuel consumption of about 125 gallons of 200 sec oil per acre of glass per day. There are a number of assumptions made in such a calculation, including heat loss in relation to wind speed and the surface area of the glasshouse, boiler efficiency, and the contribution of solar heat during the day. Nevertheless, the following formula will provide some indication of fuel requirements under average conditions:

A temperature lift of 1°C uses 25 gallons of 200 sec oil per day per acre. Based on this approximation, the following table estimates fuel consumption in Guernsey according to the temperature regime being run.

MONTH	MEAN OUTSIDE TEMPERATURE	24 HOUR MEAN TEMPERATURE		
		10°C	13°C	16°C
January	6.4°C	3300	6000	9000
February	6.2°C	3150	5600	8100
March	6.9°C	2850	5500	8100
April	8.6°C	1250	3750	6300
May	11.0°C	—	1650	4450
June	13.5°C	—	—	1950
July	15.4°C	—	—	—
August	15.7°C	—	—	—
September	14.7°C	—	—	—
October	12.1°C	—	700	3300
November	9.2°C	750	3250	6000
December	7.4°C	2400	5000	8600

TABLE 7 FUEL REQUIREMENTS IN GALLONS PER ACRE PER MONTH

Labour requirements

The freesia crop has a rather unbalanced labour requirement. There is a short peak at sowing or planting time, a low labour input for the early stages of growth, and then a high demand for picking, bunching and marketing, and again for corm lifting and glasshouse turn-round. There are two ways in which these labour peaks can be ironed out for the freesia grower. One is to grow a series of small-unit crops out of phase with each other. This has the advantage that production becomes almost year-round, and so marketing is easier. It has the disadvantage, however, that crops have to be programmed to crop at low-yield periods if the labour input is to be properly balanced through the year. A compromise is possible if crops are phased to produce over, say, a six to eight month period, avoiding the times of lowest production, and using the remaining part of the year for soil sterilisation and general maintenance work.

The second way of reducing peaks of labour requirement is to employ casual labour for picking and marketing. If such labour is readily available in the area this can be a very satisfactory arrangement, since this aspect of the labour programme represents quite a large part of the total. Also, it is work which is suitable for casual female labour, and the jobs involved are easily taught. This then leaves the general cultural work-load, most of which is more suitable for men, to be dealt with by quite a low level of permanent staff. Obviously, the labour input for a particular nursery will depend on the cultural programme employed, but the following figures give a guide for the labour requirement for the more important jobs in the freesia production cycle.

Job	**Per 1/10 Acre**
Sowing seed in beds	15.0 – 22.5 man-hours
Planting corms in beds	30.0 – 37.5 man-hours
Preparing and sowing seedling boxes	22.5 – 37.5 man-hours
Planting out seedlings	22.5 – 37.5 man-hours
Lifting corms	22.5 – 45.0 man-hours
Cleaning corms	7.5 – 15.0 man-hours

Picking:	1 to 2 man-hours per thousand stems
Bunching and packing:	1 to 3 man-hours per thousand stems.

These figures are intended to be only a guide, and actual times needed will vary widely according to circumstances and techniques. This is particularly true of the time for bunching and packing, since this depends on the marketing system in use. Various routine jobs have not been included in this list, but due allowance has to be made for these when preparing a schedule of labour requirements to go with a cropping programme. These jobs include preparing the house, tidying the crop, watering and feeding, weeding and roguing out, and pesticide application.

It is clearly impossible to assess the profitability of freesia growing here, as this depends on so many factors – e.g., production programme, cost of labour, cost of materials, fuel requirements, and market value of the blooms. All of these factors can only be properly assessed in relation to the production area in question. However, these are standard formats in which this information can be set out, so making the estimation of profitability easier. An example of this is given in Appendix 1. It is also possible to estimate labour requirements and production week by week so that man-power and marketing can be properly planned. The figures given in the example in the appendix relate to a particular crop grown in Guernsey, and obviously can be taken only as a rough guide to the way in which freesia production can be planned in a logical way.

8: Pests and Diseases

There are a number of pest and disease problems which are quite specific to freesias, and others which affect freesia crops, but which are also common to other horticultural crops. As is the case with all crops, freesias should be regularly examined for pest or disease symptoms so that control measures may be applied without delay. Early identification of problems can considerably reduce crop losses, and the time spent doing this is a very important aspect of growing freesias. The principle pests and diseases of freesias are described here, together with control measures using pesticides presently available in the UK. Elsewhere, different control measures may be applicable.

Fusarium corm rot

Fusarium corm rot is a fungal disease of freesias which causes die-back of foliage and eventually, death of the plant. The main identifying symptom is a red-brown staining in the centre of the corm, starting at the base. Within a crop the disease is spread from plant to plant through the soil and between crops the spread can be either through contaminated soil or through corms harbouring the disease. Because of the persistence of fusarium in the soil, this problem is probably the most important disease of intensive freesia culture, and every effort should be made to prevent its establishment. When the disease is identified in a growing crop the following programme will keep the spread of fusarium to a minimum:—

(1) Rogue out infected plants as soon as die-back is evident. Do this systematically right to the end of the crop — a plant with fusarium will not produce marketable blooms anyway. Remove the corm as well as the top of the plant, as this will otherwise harbour fusarium spores through the sterilisation period and provide a source of infection for the new crop.

(2) Drench the soil every three or four weeks with a solution of fungicide such as captan wettable powder.

(3) Drench the soil with the fungicide benomyl on two occasions only,

preferably not until the crop is flowering. If the disease is limited to particular areas then spot-treat these areas.

(4) The lifting operation should be carried out carefully, well before foliage has died down. This enables the grower to identify diseased areas which are only lifted once the clean corms have been removed from cleaning and treatment. Supposedly healthy stocks should be checked at lifting for fusarium by cutting through a random sample of 100.
If more than 5% are showing core staining symptoms then it would be wisest to discard the stock.

(5) If corms are being saved they should be dipped for 30 minutes in a solution of 16fl oz Difolatan and 1½lb Benomyl per 50gal immediately after cleaning and allowed to dry thoroughly before re-storing.

The limitation on the use of benomyl is recommended because it is likely that continued use of this chemical reduces its effectiveness. This is because benomyl encourages a build-up in the soil of certain bacteria which then break down the chemical before it can be taken up by the freesia plant. Other related chemicals, thiophanate methyl, carbendazim or thiabendazole, will probably be broken down in the soil in the same way, so nothing is gained by switching from benomyl to one of these alternatives.

The second aspect of the control measures needed to eliminate fusarium relates to hygiene between crops. When fusarium has been identified in a crop the following action should be taken:—

(1) When lifting, it is extremely important to be sure that all plant material is removed from the soil. Fusarium disease lying dormant within an old corm is very difficult to eradicate, and the corm itself protects the disease spores from the action of any soil sterilisation methods.

(2) The greenhouse soil should be kept moist after lifting the old crop and until soil sterilisation takes place. This will prevent the fungus from entering the dormant phase and so being more resistant to sterilisation.

(3) Soil sterilisation should be as thorough as possible. Steaming is the most effective single method for control of fusarium, but it is essential to reach all soil which may at any time come into contact with a subsequent freesia crop.

(4) Chemical sterilants, such as metham-sodium and chloropicrin give some degree of control of fusarium. Perhaps the most certain soil sterilisation technique is to use one of these chemical sterilants and follow this at a suitable interval by steaming.

(5) Methyl bromide gassing gives some control of fusarium, but it is unlikely to provide adequate sterilisation where the level of infection in the soil is high.

Virus

The following viruses affect freesias:

(1) Yellow Bean Mosaic. This causes pale flecking and striping on the leaves, and can also produce symptoms in the flowers, in which the petals are distorted, or the buds fail to open properly.
(2) Freesia Mosaic Virus. This shows no leaf symptoms, but produces light or dark flecking and colour-breaking in the flowers, and also marking on the bracts.

These two viruses are not soil-borne, but are transmitted from plant to plant by aphids, which must therefore be controlled whenever they are seen. Plants showing symptoms should be rogued out regularly, except in the case of mild leaf symptoms where it is not intended to retain the corms.

Transfer of virus from one season to the next is via the corms. Corms show no identifiable symptoms of virus when they are not in active growth, and so a stock which is being bought in should be examined before lifting if any virus present is to be recognised. There is no chemical method of control of virus.

Leaf necrosis

This disorder of freesias produces virus-like symptoms, but it has not yet been conclusively established that it is a virus. The visible symptoms are pale flecks on the leaves, which gradually merge and in severe cases cause the leaves to die. Some stocks of corms are particularly inclined to show leaf necrosis symptoms and if the symptoms develop early the subsequent corm harvest can be considerably reduced because of loss of green leaf area. There are no symptoms on the flowers.

Where leaf necrosis and freesia mosaic virus both become established in a freesia plant, the symptoms are greatly intensified, the plant generally dies right back, and the corm becomes mummified.

Botrytis

This is a common fungal disease of many horticultural crops and may affect freesias in one of three ways. The opening blooms may have small pale spots, with a raised dark spot in the centre. This is caused by spores of botrytis which settle onto the buds from the air, and then begin to germinate. Botrytis bloom spotting can develop sufficiently to ruin a crop in damp conditions, and even where the level of infection is low, the spots may develop in transit to market and

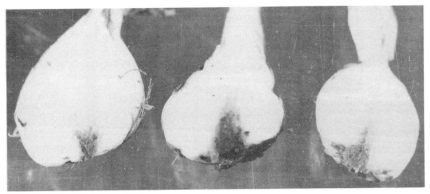

FIG 35
Fusarium is readily identified in lifted corms, as the central core of the corm is stained dark brown. Infection begins at the base of the corm, while botrytis infection, which gives a similar staining begins at the head of the corm and works its way downwards.

FIG 36
The early symptoms of freesia virus appear as pale flecking and striping on the foliage. The same symptoms occur with leaf necrosis, and in this case the flowers may open normally and show no marking or distortion.

present problems at that stage, although the blooms may have appeared clean when they were picked.

A second symptom of botrytis takes the form of die-back of the leaves. This commonly occurs on the tips of the leaves and wherever a leaf is damaged, and is usually accompanied by the 'grey mould' which is characteristic of botrytis. If botrytis conditions persist for any length of time, then the third symptom of the disease may develop. This starts as a rot at the base of the stem, which eventually kills the plant. This form of botrytis can travel down into the corm, which can be destroyed in this way. The infection of corms with botrytis can be distinguished from those with fusarium, in that the disease attacks from the head of the corm downwards, while fusarium infection begins at the base of the corm.

The primary method of botrytis control should always be cultural. The fungus develops and spreads in damp, humid conditions, and so every effort should be made to keep the crop dry, particularly at night. Ventilation and pipe heat should be used as necessary to provide air movement, and damping down the crop avoided. It is also possible to use fans to maintain air movement in still weather if pipe heating is not available. Watering frequency should be reduced, and carried out early in the morning on a bright day if possible. Keeping the crop well supported is particularly important, as the humid conditions under layered leaves is very conducive to the spread of botrytis, and for the same reason the crop should be kept free of weeds.

Chemical control measures can be used in addition to cultural techniques. Smoke formulations of quintozene or dicloran should be used where practicable for bloom spotting, as wet sprays tend to aggravate the situation. Regular dusting (every 7-10 days) with thiram or iprodione may also give a measure of control, and a heavy spray of benomyl or a related material will help to control basal rotting of the plants.

Corm soft rot

This disease of freesias can develop quite quickly and seriously in a production area. The main symptom is a softening of the corm, the body of which rots away and this is accompanied by an unpleasant smell characteristic of bacterial decay. In a growing crop this is followed by die-back of the whole plant. Soft rot usually spreads slowly in a growing crop, but if carried into store can develop much more rapidly during heat treatment. The cultural techniques which can be used to keep losses from these rots to a minimum are described in chapter four, and these relate mainly to making sure that the corms reach the store in a sound condition.

Root rots

The importance of a good, healthy root system has already been discussed, and because of this root rot fungi should be dealt with as necessary. If the soil is not sterilised before any particular crop, then a root drench combining zineb with a suitable copper fungicide should be applied once the plants are well

FIG 37
Small purple-brown pigmented spots may occur on flower buds as they develop. These are the sites of feeding punctures made by aphids at an earlier stage. They are also responsible for the distortion of the flower head.

established, and again when buds appear, or whenever any loss of root action is suspected. Captan and benomyl root drenches can be alternated with the zineb/copper drenches where fusarium corm rot is suspected.

Aphids

Aphids spread virus from plant to plant in freesias, apart from causing damage directly to marking or distorting the buds, and for this reason must be dealt with as soon as they are noticed. Aphids are susceptible to a wide range of chemicals, such as nicotine, dimethoate and pirimicarb, and any available formulation of a suitable aphicide may be used. A wet spray of dimethoate is particularly useful, provided the aphids have not developed resistance to this material, as it is systemic, and will give control for four to six weeks after application. Because of the risk of the development of pesticide resistance, the range of chemicals available for aphid control should be used alternately.

Bulb mite

Bulb mite attack results in patchy growth in freesia corm crops shortly after planting. The visible symptoms of mite infestation are red-brown stripes or flecks on the young growth, which are easily confused with the paler flecks of an early virus symptom. Internally, microscopic examination would reveal feeding tunnels with mites in them. Bulb mite can be controlled by a soil application of aldicarb.

Corms can also suffer badly during storage, and in this case the corms should be treated before they go into store, although the corms should be fully ripened first. Methyl bromide treatment can be used, or a temperature treatment of 43°C for 24-30 hours given.

Thrips

Thrips are a very common problem in freesias. These slender, mobile insects feed in and around the flower bracts and on the leaves, and produce small silvery flecks and stripes. The symptoms are very similar to the visible symptoms or virus, and a close examination is necessary to be certain of the cause. The flower buds often open badly, adding further to the illusion that the plants are infected with virus. Control of thrips can be with permerthrin wet spray or fog or propoxur smokes.

Root knot eelworm

This pest can occasionally occur on freesias, showing up in the crop as patches of stunted growth. When the plant is dug up, the fibrous root system shows the characteristic knotted apearance of 'club root'. Root knot eelworm will only display symptoms in the case of a heavy infestation, which will not develop when soil sterilisation is adequate. Where it is a problem, a soil drench with parathion will give good and permanent control.

Other pests

A range of other pests may occasionally be found on freesias. Generally speaking, these are common to many other crops, and control measures are therefore well-known. These include springtails, centipedes, caterpillars, whitefly, slugs, snails, rats and mice. One pest occasionally found on freesia crops, and specific to it, is the freesia maggot. This is the larval stage of the fly *Delia cilicrura*, which lays its eggs in soil with a high organic content. The eggs hatch, and the maggots eat the freesia roots, causing blueing of the leaves, and eventually death of the plants. A layer of an inorganic material such as sand on top of the soil will prevent egg-laying, and a soil drench of diazinon or dimethoate will kill the maggots.

Appendix 1

Sample Crop Programme
(costed 1984)

Crop Corms from seed
Area $^1/_{10}$ acre (150ft x 30ft house)
Planted First week April (not end-treated)
        36,000 corms
Start picking Week 15 – Third week July
Finish picking Week 29 – Late October
Yield (estimated) 3 stems/plant =250 boxes
        of 300 stems each
Return (estimated) £14/box (gross)

Costs	£			Returns	£		£
Corms	300			250 boxes @ £14			
Fertilisers etc	16					3500	
Pesticides	90			Less Materials			283
Soil sterilisation	245			at £1.13			
Water, electricity	40			Less Freight @ £1.34			335
Fuel	50						618
Sundries	38					2882	
	779						
Labour		1,100		Add corm value		200	
		1,879				£3082	
Glasshouse use		610					
		2,489					
Crop supports @ £1.50		120					
		£2,609		**NET PROFIT £473**			

Labour requirements (hours)

	GENERAL	PICKING ETC.	MARKETING NO. OF BOXES
Preparations	30		
Crop 1 (1st wk. April)	30 (Planting)		
Week 2	5		
3	5		
4	5		
5	5		
6	5		
7	5		
8	5		
9	5		
10	5		
11	10		
12	5		
13	10		
14	5		
15	10	10	10
16	5	15	15
17	10	20	20
18	5	20	20
19	10	25	25
20	5	30	30
21	10	35	35
22	5	35	35
23	10	30	30
24	5	30	30
25	10	30	30
26	5	25	25
27	5	25	25
28	5	15	15
29	5	15	15
30	5	360 hours	360 boxes
31	5		
32	10		
33	30 (Lifting)		
34 (end November)	10 (Cleaning)		
	300		

Appendix 2

Liquid feeds and fertilisers

The following formulae cover the types of liquid feed which would normally be used in freesia growing.

High potash	Potassium nitrate 12 oz per 100 gallons.
Medium potash	Potassium nitrate 8 oz per 100 gallons.
	Urea 2 oz per 100 gallons.
Medium nitrogen	Potassium nitrate 6 oz per 100 gallons.
	Urea 4 oz per 100 gallons.

The urea may be replaced by 1¼ times the weight of ammonium nitrate, according to availability. The required mix can be dissolved in a small (e.g. 4 pint) volume of water and diluted as needed (eg at 1 in 200) if a suitable dilution system is available.

The various feeds should be used as follows:—

High potash —	only where growth is very soft in the autumn or early winter, under low light conditions.
Medium potash —	for normal growth in autumn and winter.
Medium nitrogen —	for normal growth in spring and summer.

Base fertilisers

If soil analysis is not possible, a general recommendation for base fertilisers to be applied before planting or sowing would be:

¾ cwt carbonate of lime, plus
¾ cwt sulphate of potash per 1/10 acre.

The soil should be well soaked previously (say, 10,000 gallons per 1/10 acre) to leach out excess salts, and the lime omitted where calcium and pH are known to be high. If phosphate levels are expected to be very low, up to ½ cwt per 1/10 acre of superphosphate should be added, but this should not to be exceeded because of the risk of fluoride toxicity.

Peat culture

Where peat culture is to be tried, the following formula will make a suitable substrate. A medium-grade sphagnum moss peat should be used, and the following fertilisers added to each cubic yard.

> 10 lbs magnesian carbonate of lime
> 6 oz ureaformaldehyde
> 12 oz potassium nitrate
> 18 oz bonemeal
> 12 oz fritted trace element mix

If peat is to be recycled from a previous crop, several heavy soakings should be used to leach out nutrients and sodium, and the full levels of all the above fertilisers again used, except that, in the absence of peat analysis, only half of the lime should be used.

Appendix 3

Useful Information

Conversion factors

°C	°F
0	32
2	36
5	41
10	50
13	55
15	59
17	63
20	68
25	77
30	86

TO CONVERT

from	to	multiply by
Inches	Centimetres	2.54
Centimetres	Inches	0.39
Metres	Feet	3.28
Sq. feet	Sq. metres	0.093
Sq. metres	Sq. feet	10.76
Sq. metres	Sq. yards	1.20
Cubic metres	Cubic yards	1.31
Fluid oz.	Millilitres (c.c.)	28.4
Pints	Litres	0.57
Litres	Gallons	0.22
Ounces	Grams	28.4
Grams	Ounces	0.035
Pounds	Kilograms	0.45

Corm spacing

TRENCH WIDTH	WITHIN ROW	BETWEEN ROWS	NO. OF ROWS	CORMS PER FOOT RUN
17" (43 cm.)	3"	3"	5	20
20" (51 cm.)	3"	3"	6	24
17"	3"	2½"	6	24
20"	3"	2½"	7	28
17"	2½"	2½"	6	28
20"	2½"	2½"	7	33
17"	2½"	2½"	8	42

Calculations

Volume of a circular tank

   Multiply half the circumference (in feet) by half the diameter (in feet) by the depth (in feet). Multiply the answer by 6.25 to give the capacity in gallons.

   eg A tank with diameter 10ft, depth 8ft, and circumference 31.4ft.

$$\frac{31.4}{2} \times \frac{10}{2} \times 8 \times 6.25 = 3,920 \text{ gallons.}$$

Glasshouse volume (single span)

   Add height to ridge (in feet) to height of eaves. Divide by two, and multiply by the width (in feet) and again by the length (in feet). This gives the volume in cubic feet.

eg Height to ridge 12ft. Height to eaves 6ft.
Length 150ft. Width 30ft.

$$\frac{12 + 6}{2} = 9 \times 150 \times 30 = 40,500 \text{ cubic feet.}$$